# STYLE AT LARGE

CAROL RASMUSSEN NOBLE

# STYLE AT

## Knitting Designs

*Martingale*
& C O M P A N Y

# LARGE

## *for Real Women*

## Dedication

### To my mother

Style at Large:
Knitting Designs for Real Women
© 2003 by Carol Rasmussen Noble

**Martingale®**
& COMPANY

Martingale & Company
20205 144th Avenue NE
Woodinville, WA 98072-8478
www.martingale-pub.com

Printed in China
08 07 06 05 04 03      8 7 6 5 4 3 2 1

**Library of Congress Cataloging-in-Publication Data**

Noble, Carol R. (Carol Rasmussen)
 Style at Large : knitting designs for real women /
Carol Rasmussen Noble.
    p.   cm.
 ISBN 1-56477-490-2
 1. Knitting—Patterns.   2. Sweaters.   I. Title
 TT820.N67 2003
746.43'20432—dc21

                              2003008954

## Credits

PRESIDENT: *Nancy J. Martin*
CEO: *Daniel J. Martin*
PUBLISHER: *Jane Hamada*
EDITORIAL DIRECTOR: *Mary V. Green*
MANAGING EDITOR: *Tina Cook*
TECHNICAL EDITOR: *Karen Costello Soltys*
COPY EDITOR: *Karen Koll*
DESIGN DIRECTOR: *Stan Green*
ILLUSTRATOR: *Robin Strobel*
COVER DESIGNER: *Stan Green*
TEXT DESIGNER: *Trina Stahl*
FASHION PHOTOGRAPHER: *John Hamel*
PHOTOGRAPHER'S ASSISTANT: *Troy Schnyder*
FASHION STYLIST: *Susan Huxley*
HAIR AND MAKEUP: *Colleen Kobrick*
STUDIO PHOTOGRAPHER: *Brent Kane*

## Mission Statement

*Dedicated to providing quality products and service
to inspire creativity.*

# CONTENTS

# INTRODUCTION

*I* AM A KNITTER. I'm also a large woman. Over the years I have become disillusioned with knitting books and magazines in which the only patterns large enough for me are those for men's sweaters. We are lovely. We do not have to wear only baggy garments or only solid colors. So I decided to write a book. *Style at Large* is basically a collection of knitting patterns for women of medium to large size: that is, sweaters with finished chest measurements ranging from 44 to 62 inches.

For many years I have been designing sweaters for myself, my relatives, and my friends. I am not interested in faddish clothes that have the wrong lines for me. I look for classic chic. And that is just what I am offering you in these designs.

You may wonder about my bright or complex colors. My background is in textile collecting, and I fell in love with color in clothing early in my adult life, in the high Andes of Peru and Bolivia, where I traveled the backcountry with my geologist husband. So forget the stereotypes. Large women can wear color. This is one of my design principles.

Because the complexities of color intrigue me, I am very fond of hand-painted or hand-dyed yarns. They offer so many options and benefits compared to commercially produced yarn, and they are so beautiful. Color in a garment of hand-painted variegated or heather yarn has a life and mystery all its own. The blending colors tend to blur the harsh lines of the garment and focus attention on the knitted fabric itself rather than the shape beneath it. Combine this vision of color with classic lines and the result is elegance. With this guideline in mind, even a stripy variegated yarn can be made suitable and beautiful for large sizes.

I learned to knit from my mother when I was a little girl, and by my teenage years I was experimenting with shape and color and perfecting my technical skills. Now I am a knitwear designer and expert knitter who began to knit and sell custom designs in 1980 when I was in graduate school, both to exercise my creativity and to support my yarn habit. Along the way, I learned some design tricks that make my patterns special, and I detail the figure-flattering aspects of each design along with the project directions.

*Style at Large* has something for everyone—I hope you will be able to find yourself in it. I like to think of my designs as works in progress, so don't be hesitant to experiment with other yarns that give the correct gauge, and please use your own sense of color to make a stunning garment that both looks great and makes a statement for you. We are beautiful, so explore the possibilities!

*Carol Rasmussen Noble*

Susan Bates®
"Knit-Chek"™

mm SIZES
KNITTING
NEEDLE SIZES
CROCHET HOOK
SIZES

STITCH GAUGE
KNIT OR CROCHET
A 3 INCH SQUARE SWATCH.
PLACE THE KNIT CHECK OVER IT
COUNT THE NUMBER OF STITCHES
AND NUMBER OF ROWS PER INCH.
IF MORE OR LESS THAN SPECIFIED
TRY LARGER OR SMALLER
NEEDLES UNTIL YOU HAVE THE
REQUIRED NUMBER OF STITCHES
AND ROWS

INCH & CM RULE
ROWS & STITCHES TO THE INCH GAUGE
KNITTING NEEDLE, CROCHET HOOK & mm GAUGE

NO. 14099 SUSAN BATES, INC. GREENVILLE, SOUTH CAROLINA, 29615

# KNITTING TIPS AND TECHNIQUES

WRITING A KNITTING book provides a wonderful forum for a knitter such as myself who has definite ideas and loves to share them. I urge you to read this section before starting any of the designs in the book and refer back to it during knitting. I am going to chat here about what tricks of the trade work especially well for me. My hope is that you'll find this advice useful and that you'll be able to incorporate a new trick or two into your own knitting repertoire.

## Tools of the Trade

**Straight needles are best.** First, I would like to caution you against using circular needles in place of straight needles to knit back and forth. While some knitters prefer circular needles, I find that with their different diameters at needle tip and cord, they simply do not hold the tension evenly enough at any size. It may seem more convenient to use them, but you will get a tighter, smoother, more even surface with straight needles. I don't even like to use circular needles for knitting in the round. Rather, I prefer to use double-pointed (dp) needles for almost all projects, including Fair Isle knitting, which I do a lot of. I find 16" and 11" circular needles to be especially hard to work with and always use double points in place of them. Once you master the double-pointed technique, the knitting progresses just as quickly.

With that said, I do want to offer a note about medical conditions affecting the hand: I have rheumatoid arthritis, and I knit for at least several hours every day. My rheumatologist tells me that knitting is one of the best exercises I can do for my hands. If you have carpal tunnel syndrome or tendonitis, however, your choices of needle size and type may be limited. Try quieting your hand and wrist movement, and use the tools that work best for you. But please, keep on knitting.

**The best needles for you.** If you tend to knit tightly, use metal needles because the yarn will slip easily, whereas if you tend to knit loosely, use bamboo needles because the yarn will cling more to bamboo. Exotic wood and plastic needles fall somewhere in between. Remember that bamboo and plastic needles are flexible, and that wood needles will break if stressed.

I find flexibility to be very important in a needle because it allows the needle rather than my joints to take the stress of movement. You can quiet your hand movements and loosen your grip, both of which lead to pain-free knitting. Also watch out for exotic woods—they are pretty, but they splinter. And when I knit fine lace, where tension is very important, I use needles no longer than 10", because this gives the best control over my stitches and the piece as a whole.

**Tips on choosing yarns.** When I choose yarns, I try to match the characteristics of the yarn—twist, stretch, loft, strength, and surface—to whatever pattern I am knitting. I could go on about this forever, having learned mostly from my own mistakes, but I won't. You have to learn from your own successes and mistakes what works for you. Nothing is worse than investing time, money, and commitment in a project that doesn't turn out the way you would like. So seek advice if you're unsure, but don't ignore your own knowledge and intuition. In this book I have tried to suggest suitable yarn alternatives for all of the patterns.

**The importance of gauge.** Gauge is extremely important and highly individualistic; needle size is less relevant. Make sure that you do adequate gauge swatches before starting a project. Don't worry about what you should be doing or what the directions call for—do what works for you.

The classic way to determine your gauge is to knit a 20 stitch by 20 row piece. Then measure

the width and divide the number of stitches by the number of inches to get the stitches per inch. For example, if 20 stitches measures 4 inches, 20 divided by 4 equals 5 stitches per inch. Repeat the process with rows and the length of the piece. If the gauge is not as specified in the pattern, you should change your needle size. For a pattern stitch, knit a swatch containing two or three horizontal and vertical pattern repeats, count the stitches and rows, and do the arithmetic in the same manner as above.

**Don't forget markers.** When working lace or cables, markers are extremely helpful. Place them between cable sections or lace repeats. That way, your counting is simplified and it is much easier to catch mistakes early, especially things such as dropped yarn overs. Markers help you visualize. There are many types on the market—I prefer rubber markers because they grip the needle—or make your own out of a short length of smooth, contrasting yarn using a slipknot.

## Favorite Techniques

**Knots for durability.** I am not a knitter who abhors knots. I like my knitting to be durable enough to hold together throughout use and repeated washings, so I always tie on threads, even in lace. But do not use square knots, which are notorious for slipping apart. I always use a slipknot, as shown at the top of page 13. I have found that if you weave in your ends with the proper amount of tension, neither the doubling nor the knot will show on the surface, so you don't need to end your yarn at the beginning of a row.

**The Noble Neck.** This brings me to the Noble Neck. I hate loose, sloppy necks. For this reason, I have devised a neck based on ratios instead of number of stitches. No matter what size or yarn, the ratio will let you produce a perfect neck every time for any neck width or depth.

An unfinished neck has four basic areas—the front bind off, the back bind off, and the two diagonal edges (which may be slightly curved) that connect the bind offs (see diagram). I pick up one out of every two stitches on the diagonals, two out of every three stitches on the front bind off, and three out of every four stitches on the back bind off. The actual number of stitches picked up is immaterial, except when you need to balance a pattern repeat.

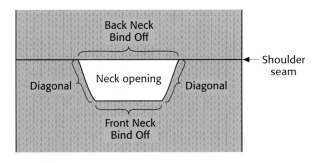

To balance a repeat of a certain number of stitches, you may need to pick up or drop extra stitches. I always make this accommodation at the left shoulder seam, although you can also use the right shoulder seam if necessary. First I do the pick up, and then make any needed adjustment on the first row by either knitting two together or increasing a stitch. Usually in making the adjustment I add stitches rather than decrease stitches because it fills out the edge. This way, no additional holes are made. Consult a basic knitting reference for making standard increases and decreases.

A problem that plagues sweater necks is the appearance of holes along the join with the body. It's very easy to avoid this problem, however, if you twist each of your picked-up stitches as you work the first row (see diagram below). This method will produce a smooth, tight join. It is also good for picking up stitches on the front bands of a cardigan, for fingers or thumbs in gloves and mittens, for picking up sleeve edge stitches for Fair Isle, or for picking up slipped stitches on a lace edge. The basic idea is to close the gap by producing a herringbone. When working necks (or anything) in the round on double-pointed needles, make sure to pull the yarn up extra tightly at the needle change to avoid a line of loose stitches.

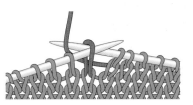

Knit or purl through back of stitch on pick-up row to create a herringbone effect and avoid the appearance of holes along the join edge.

**Holding stitches.** You will notice that on some patterns I call for putting the shoulder stitches on a spare needle instead of a stitch holder. This is only done with shoulders that are to be joined with a three-needle bind off, which requires that the spare stitches be on needles to work. For other, smaller areas, stitch holders can certainly be used. My personal preference, however, is to use a crochet hook to put the spare stitches on a loop of smooth, tightly twisted waste yarn and tie it off in a loop. Holders are awkward to knit around, and many times using them requires extra steps to get the stitch transferred back onto the needles so they are going in the correct direction.

I also highly recommend binding off front neck and back neck stitches, rather than putting them on any sort of holder. This gives a stable, non-stretchy edge that will keep the neck fitting as it is supposed to through much wear and washing.

**Front bands.** My preferred method for doing front bands is to pick up stitches on the vertical edge and then knit them outward. I pick up three out of every four stitches on the edge and twist each of them on the first row as described for "The Noble Neck" on page 13. The only difference is that if you need to make an adjustment in the number of stitches, do your knit two together or increases evenly spaced in the body of the band, not at either end. Remember that buttonholes go on the right front for women and the left front for men. Also, always bind off loosely in pattern.

**Easy buttonholes.** My recommended buttonhole is simple. It does not involve binding off and casting on, it leaves no gaps or loops, and it accommodates every size button and thickness of yarn. It is a four-stitch round buttonhole done over two rows, as shown below. When you get to within two stitches of your buttonhole placement on the right side: knit two together, double yarn over, knit two together. Continue in pattern.

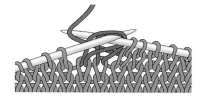

Knit 2 stitches together.

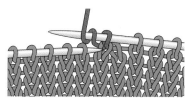

Double Yarn Over

On the reverse row for these four stitches: work one stitch in pattern, knit into first loop of double yarnover, purl into second loop of double yarnover, work one stitch in pattern. When you come to these four stitches on the next right-side row, work them in pattern. Work the buttonholes on the middle two rows of your front band. (You will need an even number of rows on your front band.)

Top and bottom buttonholes should be placed ½" from the top and bottom edges. Button spacing should be no closer than 2" and no farther apart than 3", unless you are trying for a special effect.

If you do the neckband of a cardigan first, and then knit the front bands along the total length, it is easy to plan your buttonholes. I always draw a simple schematic diagram and use a calculator to figure out how to evenly space whatever number of buttons I have to work with.

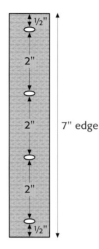

If you knit the front bands first and then the neckband, make sure to allow one button for the neckband, where you will need to place an additional buttonhole. All buttonholes will be worked horizontally, which means the neckband buttonhole will appear vertical in the finished garment, as shown below.

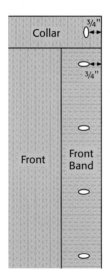

**Buttons.** When sewing buttons on the band opposite the buttonhole band, place them closer to the sweater edge than to the outside edge of the band. This way, you will get a nice balanced closure.

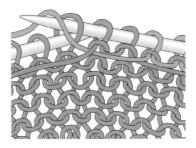

**Short-row shaping.** Sometimes I use short rows for shaping. Adding short rows is similar to adding darts on a sewn garment. They help provide a better fit for larger bustlines or a fuller roll on a collar, as in the sweater shown opposite. The principle is quite simple. You knit a partial row and then knit (or purl) back to help build up the knitted fabric at one edge as opposed to adding a complete row. Refer to the diagram for a schematic. Keep in mind that short rows have to be done in pairs to get you back to where you started.

**Changing colors.** In pure intarsia, all colors are discontinuous, meaning each is worked separately and then, each time the color changes, the two strands of yarn are wrapped around each other at the color join.

In contrast, in Fair Isle knitting, all colors are continuous, with each color yarn being brought across the whole surface on the wrong side of the work. The colors that aren't being knit are stranded loosely behind the knitted colors.

Slip stitch as if to purl. Move yarn to front of work and slip stitch back to left needle.

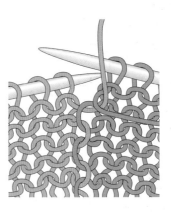

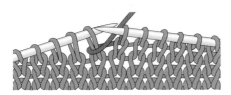

Move yarn to back of work. Turn.

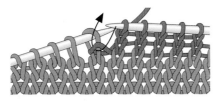

On the final row, knit bar (wrap) and stitch together.

I recommend a combination of these two techniques to do the color work in the Sunset Blocks and Mohair Cable pullovers (pages 39 and 45, respectively). Keep the main background color continuous and add discontinuous yarns (on bobbins if you choose) at each discrete color area. When knitting the color area, strand the main color loosely behind the color block area (called a "float"), and then pick up the main color again by itself in the next area. It is easier to work this way, and the piece will stretch much less.

**Three-needle bind off (3-needle BO).**
Another technique I like is the three-needle bind off for shoulders. I hate shoulders that stretch all out of shape, so I never graft them, and in my own personal knitting I never sew them. A three-needle bind off (see diagrams) gives stability to the join and keeps the shoulder and neck where they should be when you wear the sweater. If you do the three-needle bind off with right sides together, you will get a seam ridge on the inside of the sweater.

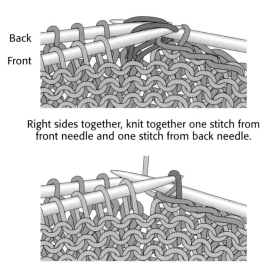

Right sides together, knit together one stitch from front needle and one stitch from back needle.

Bind off.

If you do the three-needle bind off with wrong sides together, the seam ridge is on the outside of the sweater—my personal preference. I like to use it as a design feature. For example, you can introduce a second color as the binding yarn. Just keep in mind that the front and back of the three-needle-bind-off seam look different, so make sure you use the same procedure on both shoulders. Binding off from the front or the back is your choice. You can use the same size or smaller needles to hold the stitches, and I always use a smaller needle for the working needle.

**Washing and blocking.** I would like to offer some of my views on washing and blocking. Every yarn works up differently. If you are not sure how the piece can best be finished or fulled, work some swatches and try different methods on them to see the results. I have given suggested washing and blocking instructions for each piece in this book. Most yarns respond well to a little blocking, even if it is just a light steaming. Steaming works very well in evening out the surface of color work. That said, never steam ribbings or textured patterns because it will flatten and stretch them.

My preferred method of washing is to use lukewarm water for bath and rinse. Baby shampoo is gentler than detergents, which often will cause colors to run or will harden delicate fibers. I always let a sweater soak at least for an hour or two, typically overnight. That way it literally cleans itself and doesn't require scrubbing or squeezing, which can felt the yarn. On the other hand, if you are knitting with yarn that has large unspun areas, such as chunky, thick and thins, or

Lopi, you want to try to felt the yarn at least a little to make the garment more durable. For most yarns, it is a good idea to put them through the spin cycle of your washer so that they are drier for blocking and won't droop with the weight of the water.

But some knitting—particularly pieces that need to be pulled, stretched, and pinned to shape—requires being blocked soaking wet. Do this before sewing the pieces together. If you need to block an extremely delicate piece, such as lace, wet it in your hand with a spray bottle and keep spraying it as you proceed with the blocking. I don't have any special blocking forms—I just lay out or pin out the pieces on the carpet face-up using T pins. To keep pets and kids away, the blocked piece can be covered with a towel or placed in a room where the door can be shut so the garment can remain undisturbed until dry.

**Hand-painted yarns.** The colors in hand-painted yarns commonly run. Test a piece of yarn or a small swatch before leaving a sweater to soak, especially if it is variegated. In many cases the exhaust dye comes out after a few washings. And, if you notice that exhaust dye is rubbing off onto your hands or needles as you knit, you can soak the piece itself and any unused skeins in a bath of white vinegar and lukewarm water to set the dye and then leave them very slightly stretched to dry.

A final word on using hand-painted yarns: Each dye lot—indeed each skein—will be slightly different. Don't be put off by this. Simply use the yarn's variations as a design feature to enrich the color palette of your garment.

So much for my tips and techniques. I hope you have learned a few things that you will use to improve your project. But ultimately, the craft of knitting is highly individual, and you should follow your own inclinations. Happy knitting!

# SWEATER DESIGNS

# JELLYBEANS RIBBED TURTLENECK

## Designer's Notes

A RIBBED TURTLENECK may at first glance seem unsuitable for a large woman, but that's not the case here. This sweater is designed with long vertical rows of rib, which soften the horizontal effect of variegated yarn and therefore make the body look thinner. The design creates a body-skimming rib with plenty of ease that is meant to be worn unstretched. The three-fold loose turtleneck focuses attention on the vertical line of the neck and frames the face.

Variegated yarn can tend to knit into horizontal stripes, but you can easily modify the effect by periodically cutting out a 10" to 15" section of yarn, and then retying the yarn ends to change the color repeat. Worked in this way, the color forms allover discrete shapes rather than bold horizontal stripes. Also, this Filaro yarn tends to blotch rather than stripe, and the pattern it creates will be different for each sweater size. Regardless of which size you make, you can expect the colors to stripe on the neck.

If you prefer a more subdued look, choose a subtle hand-painted variegation in your favorite colors. The sweater would also be beautiful in a heather or solid color, but keep in mind that it is designed for mohair only.

## Finished Measurements

To FIT SIZES: Medium (Large, XL, 1X, 2X)
FINISHED BUST: 44 (48, 52, 56, 60)"
FINISHED LENGTH: 24 (24, 25, 25, 26)"

## Materials

♦ 8 (9, 10, 11, 12) skeins of Filaro 12-ply
   mohair (74% mohair, 24% wool, 2%
   nylon: 109 yds/50 g skein) from Cherry
   Tree Hill Yarns, color Jellybeans
♦ Size 8 (5.0 mm) needles, or size to obtain
   gauge
♦ Set of size 8 (5.0 mm) dp needles

## Gauge

4 sts = 1"; 5 rows = 1" in rib pattern

## Rib Pattern

*(2 st, 2 row repeat)*

**Row 1:** (RS) *K1, P1, repeat from * to end.
**Row 2:** (WS) *P1, K1, repeat from * to end.

## Back

♦ CO 88 (96, 104, 112, 120) sts.
♦ Work in rib patt for 23½ (23½, 24½, 24½,
   25½)", ending on WS.
♦ On next RS row, work 28 (32, 34, 38, 40)
   sts in patt; attach second ball of yarn and
   BO 32 (32, 36, 36, 40) sts; work 28 (32,
   34, 38, 40) sts in patt.
♦ BO 2 sts at each neck edge once. Stitches
   remaining on each shoulder: 26 (30, 32,
   36, 38) sts; finished neck: 36 (36, 40, 40,
   44) sts.
♦ Work even until back measures 24 (24, 25,
   25, 26)". BO shoulders loosely.

## Front

♦ Work as for back until front measures 21
   (21, 22, 22, 23)", ending on WS.
♦ On next RS row, work in patt 32 (36, 38,
   42, 44) sts; attach second ball of yarn and
   BO next 24 (24, 28, 28, 32) sts; work in
   patt 32 (36, 38, 42, 44) sts.
♦ At each neck edge BO 2 sts twice, then
   1 st twice. Each shoulder will have
   26 (30, 32, 36, 38) sts.
♦ Work even in patt, working each shoulder
   with its own ball of yarn until front measures 24 (24, 25, 25, 26)". BO all shoulder
   sts loosely.

## Sleeves

- CO 30 (32, 34, 36, 38) sts.
- Work in rib patt for 4 rows.
- On fifth row and every subsequent fourth row (RS), inc 1 st each edge 23 (24, 25, 26, 27) times. Sleeve will have total of 76 (80, 84, 88, 92) sts.
- Work even in patt until sleeve measures 19½, (20, 20½, 21, 21½)". BO all sts loosely.

## Neck

See "The Noble Neck" on page 13 before picking up stitches.

- Sew shoulder seams.
- With dp needles, pick up neck sts as follows: starting at left front shoulder, pick up 1 of every 2 sts on diagonal neck edges; 2 of every 3 sts on front neck BO; and 3 of every 4 sts on back neck BO. Because rib patt repeat is 2 sts, you will need a multiple of 2 for total neck sts. If you need to dec or inc number of sts, make adjustment at left shoulder. Usually in making the adjustment I add stitches rather than decrease stitches because it fills out the edge. Work neck in round on dp needles for 12", or length to suit (neck rolls over twice). BO all sts in patt very loosely.

## Finishing

- No blocking is necessary. Do not steam or press ribbing.
- Measure 14½ (14, 14½, 14, 14½)" from the bottom edge on each piece and pin mark this distance on each side edge of the front and back. Sew the sleeve tops to the sweater between these markings.
- Sew the underarm and side seams; weave in ends.

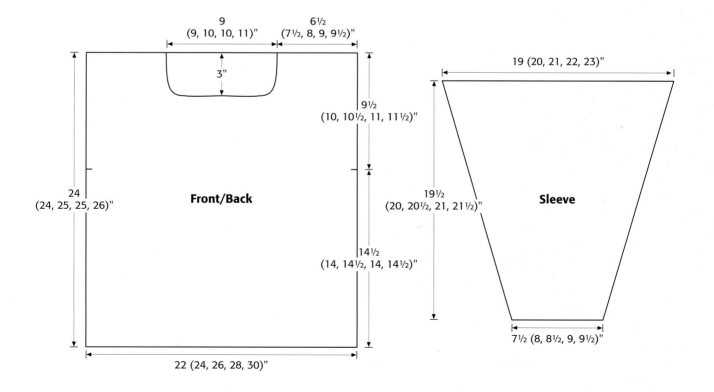

# VELVETY VEST IN CHUNKY CHENILLE

## Designer's Notes

THIS ROOMY VEST knits up very easily in chunky chenille yarn, making it suitable for beginners. Designed with a wide shoulder line that gives the illusion of being wider than the hips, and with a very generous armhole, it is attractive on even the largest woman and can be sized accordingly. The vertical line of the simple knit-purl stitch pattern is thinning. It can be easily made longer, shorter, or fuller to suit any individual.

I used Plush from Cherry Tree Hill Yarns, but it looks good in any type of chunky chenille. I chose a hand-painted sold color, but a heather or variegated colorway would work just as well. Choose a thicker, fuller chenille for best results.

## Finished Measurements

To FIT SIZES: Medium (Large, XL, 1X, 2X)
FINISHED BUST: 46 (50, 54, 58, 62)"
FINISHED LENGTH: 24 (24, 25, 25, 26)"

## Materials

♦ 24 (32, 36, 40, 48) oz total weight of Plush from Cherry Tree Hill in purple, or any chunky-weight chenille yarn that gives gauge
♦ Size 10 (6.0 mm) needles, or size to obtain gauge

## Gauge

2 st = 1"; 4 rows = 1" in pattern

## Pattern Stitch

*(2 st, 2 row repeat)*

**Row 1:** (RS) *P1, K1, repeat from * to end.
**Row 2:** (WS) Purl across.

## Back

♦ CO 46 (50, 54, 58, 62) sts.
♦ Work K2P2 ribbing for 2", ending on WS.
♦ On next RS row, begin patt and work until back measures 13 (13, 14, 14, 14)", ending on WS.
♦ BO 2 sts at beg of next 2 rows.
♦ Dec 1 st each armhole edge on RS 2 times; 38 (42, 46, 50, 54) sts. Work even until armhole measures 10 (10, 10, 10, 11)", ending on WS.
♦ Work 11 (13, 15, 16, 17) sts; attach second ball of yarn and BO next 16 (16, 16, 18, 20) sts; work 11 (13, 15, 16, 17) sts. Work even until back measures 24 (24, 25, 25, 26)".
♦ Place shoulder stitches on spare needle for 3-needle BO.

## Front

♦ Work as for back until armhole measures 6½ (6½, 6½, 6½, 7½)".
♦ On next RS row, work 14 (16, 18, 19, 20) sts; attach second ball of yarn and BO 10 (10, 10, 12, 14) sts; work 14 (16, 18, 19, 20) sts.

◆ Beg with next RS row, dec 1 st each neck edge 3 times (total 6 sts dec). Remaining shoulders will each have 11 (13, 15, 16, 17) sts. Work even until front measures 24 (24, 25, 25, 26)".

◆ Place shoulder stitches on spare needle for 3-needle BO.

## Finishing

◆ Do not steam block.

◆ Join shoulders with 3-needle BO, referring to page 18.

◆ Sew underarm and side seams; weave in ends.

◆ Neck and armholes require no additional finishing.

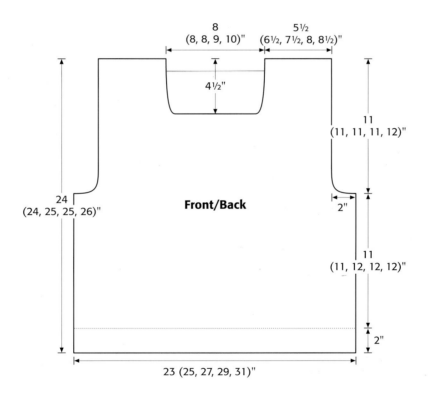

# CASHMERE-AND-SILK FITTED COWL

## Designer's Notes

THE LINES OF this dressy cowl-neck top drape gracefully. It can be worn under a business suit for a day in the office or alone as a dressy sweater. The neck folds down softly to frame the face, and the fit is neither tight nor baggy. A few strategically placed increases and decreases on the sides give the right amount of shaping to give the illusion of a waist to those of us who perhaps don't have much of one. For large midriffs, the shaping could simply be eliminated.

The square armhole has the virtue of strong geometric lines, giving the sweater a fitted look. At the same time, this detailing allows for a generous armhole, because the dovetailing of the sleeve into the opening makes a kind of gusset. While the forearm is more fitted, the upper arm is quietly generous, to allow roominess without ruining the lines of the sweater.

The combination of the allover double seed stitch pattern with a subdued hand-painted colorway is both sophisticated and thinning. The subtle colors meander over the garment like a cloud on a sunny day, drawing attention to the yarn and the garment and away from the edges of the shape beneath. For weekend wear, a more robust variegation would be fun, but you should still choose an elegant luxury yarn such as this fingering-weight cashmere-silk blend. It would also work up beautifully in a pure cashmere, merino, or merino-silk blend.

31

## Finished Measurements

TO FIT SIZES: Medium (Large, XL, 1X, 2X)
FINISHED BUST: 44 (48, 52, 56, 60)"
FINISHED LENGTH: 25½ (26, 26½, 27, 27½)"

## Materials

- 6 (7, 8, 9, 10) skeins of cashmere-silk 2-ply fingering blend (80% cashmere, 20% silk; 228 yds/50 g skein) by Cherry Tree Hill Yarns, colorway Java
- Size 2 (2.75 mm) needles, or size to obtain gauge
- Set of size 2 (2.75 mm) dp needles

## Gauge

5 sts = 1"; 8 rows = 1" in double seed st pattern

## Double Seed Stitch Pattern

*(4 st, 4 row repeat)*

**Row 1:** (RS) *K2, P2, repeat from * to end.
**Row 2:** (WS) *P2, K2, repeat from * to end.
**Row 3:** (RS) *P2, K2, repeat from * to end.
**Row 4:** (WS) *K2, P2, repeat from * to end.

## Back

- Using regular needles, CO 110 (120, 130, 140, 150) sts. Work in patt for 4", ending on WS.
- On next RS row, dec 1 st each edge, and then 1 st each RS edge every 8 rows 4 times (5 st dec each edge).
- At 9" on RS, inc 1 st each edge, and then 1 st each RS edge every 8 rows 4 times (5 st inc each edge). Cont in patt for 3", ending on WS.

- At beg of next 2 rows, BO 10 sts. Total sts: 90 (100, 110, 120, 130). Work in patt until back measures 24½ (25, 25½, 26, 26½)".
- Work 25 (27, 29, 32, 34) sts in patt; attach second ball of yarn and BO 40 (46, 52, 56, 62) sts; work in patt 25 (27, 29, 32, 34) sts.
- Working each shoulder with its own ball of yarn, dec 1 st each neck edge on following RS row twice. Total shoulder sts: 23 (25, 27, 30, 32). When back measures 25½ (26, 26½, 27, 27½)", BO all sts loosely.

## Front

- Work same as back until armhole measures 6¼ (6½, 6¾, 7, 7¼)", ending on WS.
- On next RS row, work 33 (35, 37, 40, 42) sts; attach second ball of yarn and BO 24 (30, 36, 40, 46) sts; work 33 (35, 37, 40, 42) remaining sts.
- Working each shoulder with its own ball of yarn, dec as follows for all sizes: BO 2 sts each neck edge every other row 3 times, and then dec 1 st each neck edge every other row 4 times. Total dec: 10 sts each shoulder. Total finished shoulder sts: 23 (25, 27, 30, 32).
- When armhole measures 9½ (10, 10½, 11, 11½)", BO all sts loosely.

## Sleeves

- CO 40 (40, 45, 45, 50) sts. Working in patt, on fifth and every subsequent fourth row (RS), inc 1 st each edge 27 (30, 30, 32, 32) times. Total sts: 94 (100, 105, 109, 114). Work even until sleeve measures 20½ (21, 21½, 22, 22½)". BO all sts loosely.

# Neck

See "The Noble Neck" on page 13 before picking up stitches.

♦ Sew shoulder seams.

♦ With dp needles, starting at left shoulder pick up 1 of every 2 sts on diagonal edges; 2 of every 3 sts on front neck BO; 3 of every 4 sts on back neck BO. Patt requires multiple of 4 sts. Make any necessary adjustments (inc or dec) on left shoulder. Work in patt in the round until neck measures 12" for all sizes. BO all sts very loosely in patt.

# Finishing

♦ No blocking is necessary. Do not steam, as this will flatten the pattern.

♦ Sew side and sleeve seams; weave in ends.

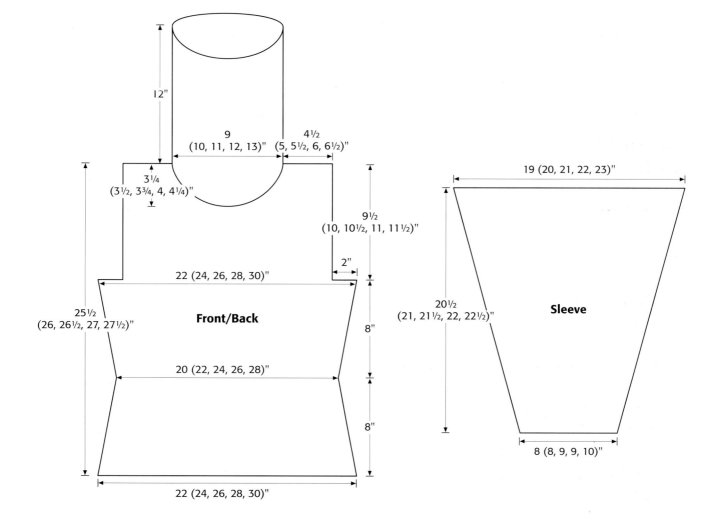

# UNSTRUCTURED PLUSH MOHAIR JACKET

## Designer's Notes

I LIKE TO wear this chic unstructured jacket with a brooch to hold it closed, but you could also use frogs, Norwegian clasps, or one or two strategically placed large buttons with loops. Try it with a contrasting leather belt or allow it to drape open naturally. The collar can be folded up or down to suit your style.

Perfect for beginners, this jacket features the simple garter stitch, and the front and back panels are each knit as one piece, including the collar. The jumbo loopy mohair knit on smaller needles produces a plush, fulled-looking fabric that hides the individual rows of stitches. In short, this is a very versatile pattern.

The drop shoulder makes for a roomy armhole. The forearms are more fitted than the upper arms to give a good line to the sleeves. The color is subtle, yet exciting. I think that this design is especially suited to hand-painted or heather yarns. Choose a mohair yarn that is very loopy and highly twisted and you'll have a garment that can be dressed up or down to grace a variety of occasions. It is really a four-season garment for much of the West and Southwest, and a three-season garment elsewhere.

## Finished Measurements

To FIT SIZES: Medium (Large, XL, 1X, 2X)
FINISHED BUST: 44 (48, 52, 56, 60)"
FINISHED LENGTH: 24 (25, 26, 27, 28)"

## Materials

◆ 5 (6, 6, 7, 7) skeins of Jumbo Loop Mohair (100% mohair, 252 yds/8 oz) from Cherry Tree Hill Yarns, colorway Gypsy Rose
◆ Size 6 (4.0 mm) needles, or size to obtain gauge

## Gauge

3.5 sts = 1"; 6 rows = 1" in garter stitch

## Back

◆ CO 77 (84, 91, 98, 105) sts.
◆ Work in garter st until back measures 24 (25, 26, 27, 28)".
◆ BO 24 (28, 31, 33, 35) sts; work 29 (28, 29, 32, 35) sts; attach second ball of yarn. BO 24 (28, 31, 33, 35) sts.
◆ Work center sts until neck measures 3½" from shoulder.
◆ BO all sts very loosely.

## Left Front

The left front tucks under the right front.

◆ CO 42 (45, 49, 52, 56) sts.
◆ Work in garter st until piece measures 24 ( 25, 26, 27, 28)". End on WS.
◆ On next RS row, BO 24 (28, 31, 33, 35) sts on left edge. Work 18 (17, 18, 19, 21) sts until collar measures 3½" above shoulder.
◆ BO all sts very loosely.

## Right Front

The right front folds over the left front.

◆ CO 49 (52, 56, 59, 63) sts.
◆ Work in garter st until front measures 24 (25, 26, 27, 28)". End on RS.
◆ At beg of next WS row (on right edge), BO 24 (28, 31, 33, 35) sts. Work remaining 25 (24, 25, 26, 28) sts until neck measures 3½" above shoulder.
◆ BO all sts very loosely.

## Sleeves

- ◆ CO 36 (38, 40, 42, 44) sts.
- ◆ Work in garter st. On fifth and every subsequent fourth row (RS), inc 1 st each sleeve edge 17 (18, 18, 19, 20) times. Total sts: 70 (74, 76, 80, 84).
- ◆ Work even until sleeve measures 17 (18, 19, 20, 21)". BO all stitches loosely.

## Blocking

Since this yarn has a double twist, the pieces may not come off the needles square. Blocking is necessary before sewing them together. Wash all four pieces by hand in lukewarm water and baby shampoo. Do not put in spin cycle of washer. Do not squeeze out excess moisture. Pieces should be blocked soaking wet. Pin out wet pieces to exact measurements given in diagrams with RS up. Do not steam or press. Allow to dry thoroughly.

## Finishing

Sew shoulder seams and neck seams with sewing thread in matching color using an overcast st on the edges. Do not pull tight enough to pucker. Full armholes measure 20 (21, 22, 23, 24)". Sew in sleeve tops and then sew side and underarm seams with overcast st in matching sewing thread.

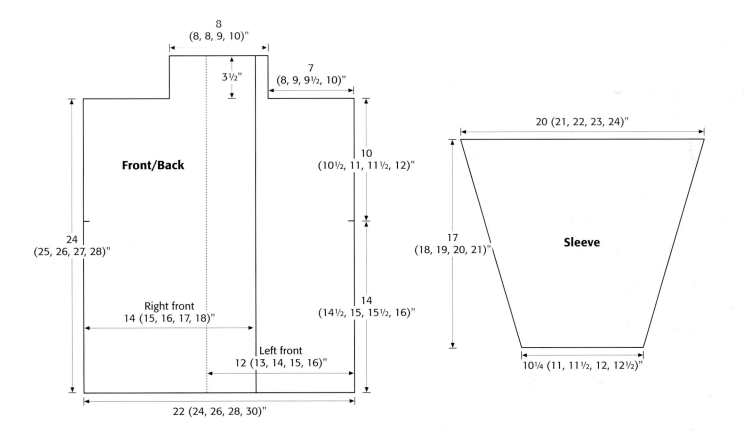

# SUNSET BLOCKS PULLOVER

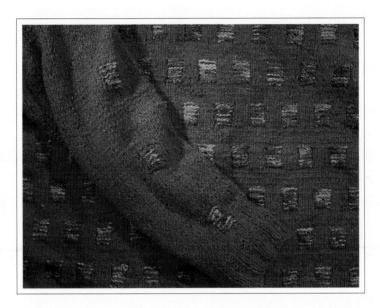

## Designer's Notes

EVERYONE LIKES AND needs a classic crewneck pullover. My version, Sunset Blocks, is a very basic shape that focuses attention on the diamond grid of boxes of brilliant color set against the rich red of the background. The eye wanders from block to block, seeing only a dance of color even though the color placement and texture is basically conservative. The sleeves add another slimming design feature, using the pattern in a single, strong, vertical line.

I chose a raw silk–wool blend for this project, but you could also use any sturdy DK-weight yarn such as wool, cotton, or blends if you don't want to incur the expense of a luxury fiber. Although I urge you to explore your own color sense, I recommend that the background be solid and the blocks variegated, and that the colors of both yarns have similar intensity. This design calls out for bright color. It is meant to be striking, but essentially casual.

Although this sweater technically calls for intarsia, it can be knit more simply by stranding the unused yarn over the opposite blocks on the two-color bands. The floats will be short. To produce a flat, unpuckered surface that allows the color and texture to shine, be careful to choose a nonstretchy yarn. Some advanced skill is required to knit this design, so I rate it for intermediate knitters. Even so, don't be intimidated; only knit and purl stitches are used.

## Finished Measurements

To FIT SIZES: Large (1X)
FINISHED BUST: 47 (55)"
FINISHED LENGTH: 26 (28)"

NOTE: *Because of the nature of the design and its large repeat, this pattern is written in only two sizes. These sizes, however, fit a lot of people.*

## Materials

♦ 5 (8) skeins of Rustic Silk from Cherry Tree Hill Yarn (80% raw silk, 20% wool; 300 yds/4 oz) in main color (MC) Red
♦ 2 (5) skeins of same yarn in contrasting color (CC) Champlain Sunset

♦ Size 6 (4.0 mm) needles, or size to obtain gauge
♦ Set of size 6 (4.0 mm) dp needles, or size to obtain gauge
♦ Two extra needles size 6 or smaller for shoulders

## Gauge

5.25 sts = 1"; 7 rows = 1" in St st

## Pattern Stitch

*(10 st, 32 row repeat; 5 st repeat for sleeves)*

See chart A Back, chart B Front, and chart C Sleeve on page 43 for pattern details.

## Back

♦ CO 124 (144) sts in MC. Work K2P2 ribbing for 2". On last WS row, inc 1 st; total stitches: 125 (145).
♦ Begin chart A, reading RS (odd-numbered) rows from left to right and WS (even-numbered) rows from right to left. You will have 12½ (14½) horizontal patt repeats across. Work in patt, using CC where indicated for 5 (5½) vertical patt repeats (160 [176] rows).
♦ Work 3 more rows in MC.
♦ On next RS row, work in MC across 42 (49) sts; attach second ball of yarn in MC and BO 41 (47) sts; work in MC across 42 (49) sts. On next RS row, dec 1 st each neck edge. Shoulders have 41 (48) sts.
♦ Work 2 more rows in MC, ending on RS, with last row worked on spare needle. Leave sts on spare needle; cut yarn. Back measures approximately 26 (28)" long.

## Front

- Work same as back but use chart B until you have completed 4½ (5) vertical patt repeats.
- Work 2 more rows patt (MC). On next RS row, work in patt across 47 (54) sts; attach second ball of yarn and BO 31 (37) sts; work in patt across 47 (54) sts.
- Cont to work each shoulder with its own ball of yarn. On next and every following RS row, dec 1 st each neck edge 6 times for both sizes. Total: 12 sts dec (6 each edge).
- Cont to work in patt until you have completed 5 (5½) vertical patt repeats. Work 8 rows MC, ending on WS, with last row worked on spare needle. Leave sts on spare needle; cut yarn. Front measures approximately 26 (28)" in length.

## Sleeves

- CO 44 (64) sts in MC. Work K2P2 ribbing for 2". On last WS row, inc 1 st; total sts: 45 (65).
- Next RS row is setup row: Work 20 (30) sts in MC; work chart C (5 sts); work 20 (30) sts in MC. AT SAME TIME inc 1 st each side on fifth and every subsequent fourth row on RS 30 times for both sizes.
- Work total 3 (4) vertical repeats of chart C, plus 24 additional patt rows, ending on WS.
- BO all sts loosely.

## Neck

See "The Noble Neck" on page 13 before picking up stitches.

- Place front and back wrong sides together and finish shoulders with 3-needle BO, referring to page 18.
- Using dp needles, pick up sts starting at left shoulder: Pick up 1 of every 2 sts on diagonal edges; pick up 2 of every 3 sts on front neck BO; pick up 3 of every 4 sts on back neck BO. Ribbing requires a multiple of 4 sts. Add or dec sts as necessary on left shoulder.
- Work K2P2 ribbing in MC for 1".
- BO all sts very loosely in rib patt.

## Finishing

- Before sewing the seams, each piece must be heavily steam blocked on reverse side and allowed to dry to achieve a flat surface. Do not steam ribbings.
- Sew rest of seams; weave in ends.

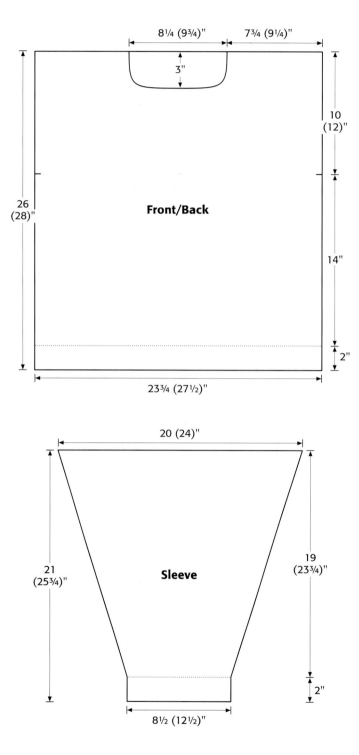

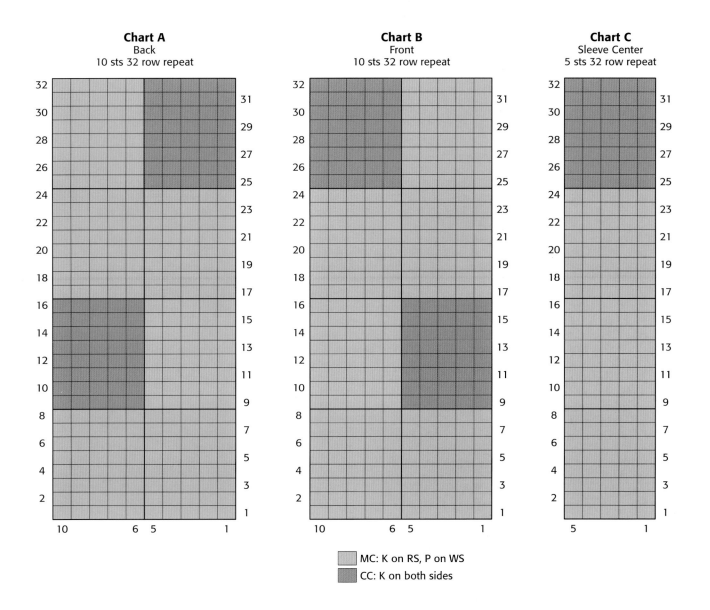

**Chart A**
Back
10 sts 32 row repeat

**Chart B**
Front
10 sts 32 row repeat

**Chart C**
Sleeve Center
5 sts 32 row repeat

MC: K on RS, P on WS
CC: K on both sides

# MOHAIR CABLE PULLOVER

## Designer's Notes

I LOVE MOHAIR. One result of my passion is this design, where mohair gives a different "twist" to the classic crewneck pullover. Verticality rules here, giving a thinning look to a fluffy, cuddly yarn. The simple cables in variegated yarn spaced over a solid background add just a dollop of intense color so that neither the color nor texture is overwhelming.

By incorporating only a center panel of strong color and texture on the sleeves, the sleeves also create a slimming effect. The sweater itself is essentially boxy in shape, so it conceals well, and would be stunning on a very large woman.

The color technique used here is intarsia—where each color is carried on a separate ball or bobbin. To simplify the knitting, you could strand the background yarn over the cable sections because the float will be short. Just take care to keep a flat surface in intarsia.

I used custom-dyed brushed mohair in periwinkle and Filaro 12-ply mohair in bubblegum, both from Cherry Tree Hill, but the design is suitable to any brand of brushed mohair. I urge you to try your own color scheme. For a casual sweater version, you could use two solid colors; for a dressier version a glitter mohair would be nice. The colors can be bright and contrasting, or subdued and understated. I would not, however, recommend anything else but brushed mohair blends for this design.

## Finished Measurements

To FIT SIZES: Medium (Large, XL, 1X, 2X)
FINISHED BUST: 46 (50, 54, 58, 62)"
FINISHED LENGTH: 24½ (25, 25½, 26, 26½)"

## Materials

+ 16 (18, 20, 22, 24) oz of Cherry Tree Hill brushed mohair in Periwinkle, or any brushed mohair or mohair blend for main color (MC)
+ 2 (2, 2, 3, 3) 50 g balls of Filaro 12-ply mohair in Bubblegum, or any brushed mohair or mohair blend in contrasting color (CC)
+ Size 8 (5.0 mm) and size 10 (6.0 mm) needles and size 8 (5.0 mm) dp needles, or sizes to obtain gauge
+ 5 bobbins (7 needed for size 2X)
+ Large cable needle

## Gauge

4 sts = 1"; 4 rows = 1" on larger needles in St st

## Cable Pattern

*(4 st, 8 row repeat for cables only)*

Twist cable on every 8th RS row.
**Odd rows 1–7:** (WS) Purl all sts.
**Even rows 2–6:** (RS) Knit all sts.
**Row 8:** (RS) Slip 2 sts to cable needle and drop to back; knit next 2 sts; pick up and knit 2 sts from cable needle (C4B).

## Back

+ On size 8 needles, CO 84 (92, 100, 108, 116) sts in MC. Work K2P2 ribbing for 2". On last WS row, inc 8 sts evenly spaced across row, all sizes. Sts on needle: 92 (100, 108, 116, 124).
+ Change to size 10 needles. Set up row: K12 (16, 20, 24, 12) sts in MC; (K4 CC, K12 MC) 4 (4, 4, 4, 6) times; K4 CC; K 12 (16, 20, 24, 12) MC.
+ On WS, purl in appropriate color across. (Note: in intarsia, twist the yarns at the color joins to avoid holes. See "Changing colors" on page 17 for details.)
+ **Row 3:** (RS) Make this your first cable row; thereafter cross cables every eighth RS row. Making sure to twist the yarn at each color change, work in patt until back measures: 24 (24½, 25, 25½, 26)".
+ On next RS row, work in patt 30 (33, 36, 38, 41) sts; attach new ball of MC and BO 32 (34, 36, 40, 42) sts; work in patt 30 (33, 36, 38, 41) sts.
+ Work each side with its separate ball of yarn in patt for ½", all sizes. BO all sts loosely.

## Front

+ Work same as back until front measures 21¾ (22, 22¼, 22½, 22¾)".
+ On next RS row, work in patt 35 (38, 41, 43, 46) sts; attach new ball of MC and BO 22 (24, 26, 30, 32) sts; work across 35 (38, 41, 43, 46) sts.
+ On next RS and each following RS row, dec 1 st at each neck edge 5 times, all sizes. Cont to work sides separately in patt until piece measures 24½ (25, 25½, 26, 26½)". BO all sts loosely.

## Sleeves

✦ On size 8 needles, CO 38 (40, 42, 44, 46) sts. Work in K2P2 ribbing for 2". On last WS row, inc 4 sts evenly spaced across, all sizes: 42 (44, 46, 48, 50) sts.

✦ Change to size 10 needles. Setup row: K19 (20, 21, 22, 23) sts MC; K4 sts CC; K19 (20, 21, 22, 23) sts MC. Cross cable on third and every following eighth RS row. At same time, inc 1 st each edge in MC on fifth and every subsequent fourth row on RS 17 (18, 19, 20, 21) times. Total sts: 76 (80, 84, 88, 92).

✦ When sleeve measures 19 (19½, 20, 20½, 21)", BO all sts loosely.

## Neck

See "The Noble Neck" on page 13 before picking up stitches.

✦ Sew shoulder seams.

✦ Pick up neck sts on size 8 dp needles starting at left shoulder. On diagonal edges, pick up 1 of every 2 sts; on front neck BO, pick up 2 of every 3 sts; on back neck BO, pick up 3 of every 4 sts. Ribbing is 4 st repeat, so make adjustment in number of sts if needed on left shoulder.

✦ Work K2P2 ribbing in MC for 1½". BO all sts very loosely.

## Finishing

✦ Do not steam or block.

✦ Sew seams; weave in ends.

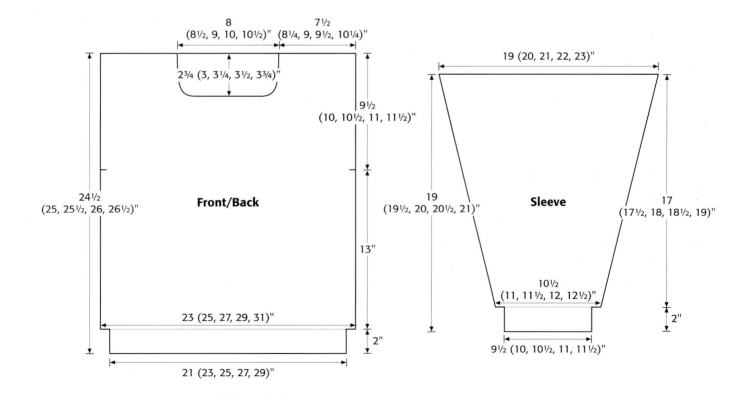

# CHECKERBOARD
## CARDIGAN

## Designer's Notes

EVERY WOMAN NEEDS a warm, classic cardigan for fall and winter. The Checkerboard Cardigan is my version. I wanted a subtle, easy-to-knit, knit-purl pattern, in muted colorways. I chose a very warm, soft worsted blend of merino wool and opossum fur, but really any worsted-weight wool or wool-blend could be used. If you choose a blend, I recommend that wool be the major component.

This design is perfect for hand-painted yarns, whether you choose a classic, muted variegation or a bright, showy one. The colorway shown—Birches—looks and feels like winter to me. But I can also see this sweater knit in autumn leaves colors. The variegated color and checkerboard repeat draw the eye into the sweater and de-emphasize the size and edges of the garment. The long length and general roominess conceal bust, midriff, and hips. The pattern is written in three sizes, and is meant to be worn loose, with lots of ease.

Another design feature is that the combined fronts are somewhat wider than the back for ease of wearing on a large figure. The seed-stitch bands replace traditional ribbing with an overall small-patterned, textured surface that softens the edges and does not pull in like ribbing does. This sweater is suitable for advanced beginner and intermediate knitters.

# Finished Measurements

To FIT SIZES: Large (1X, 2X)
FINISHED BUST: 47 (53½, 59½)"
FINISHED LENGTH: 26"

# Materials

◆ 16 (18, 22) skeins Possum Paints worsted (80% merino wool, 20% opossum fur, 109 yds per 50 g skein) from Cherry Tree Hill Yarn, colorway Birches
◆ Ten 1"-diameter buttons, or number to suit
◆ Size 7 (4.5 mm) needles, or size to obtain gauge
◆ 3 extra needles same size or smaller

# Gauge

5 sts = 1"; 7 rows = 1" in checkerboard pattern

# Stitch Patterns

## SEED STITCH
*(For even number of stitches: multiple of 2 sts)*

**All rows:** *K1, P1; repeat from * to end.

## CHECKERBOARD PATTERN
*(8 st repeat plus 1 st; 12 row repeat)*

See the chart on page 53 for the checkerboard pattern.

# Back

◆ CO 109 (125, 141) sts. Work in seed st patt for 2". On last WS row, inc 4 sts evenly spaced, all sizes. Total sts: 113 (129, 145).
◆ Begin checkerboard patt, reading RS (odd-numbered) rows from right to left, and WS (even-numbered) rows from left to right. Follow chart. There will be 14 (16, 18) horizontal patt repeats plus 1 st. Continue in patt until 13½ vertical patt repeats have been completed, ending on WS.
◆ On next RS row, work 40 (46, 51) sts; attach second ball of yarn and BO 33 (37, 43) sts; work 40 (46, 51) sts.
◆ On next RS row, dec 1 st each neck edge 1 time, all sizes. Shoulders will have 39 (45, 50) sts. Work both shoulders on separate balls of yarn in patt until 14 vertical patt repeats have been completed and back measures 26".
◆ End on WS, putting sts from shoulders on spare needle for 3-needle BO.

## Left Front

- CO 55 (63, 71) sts. Work in seed st patt for 2". On last WS row, inc 2 sts evenly spaced for all sizes. Total sts: 57 (65, 73).
- Begin checkerboard patt, reading chart as for back. There will be 7 (8, 9) horizontal repeats plus 1 st. Work even until 12½ vertical patt repeats have been completed, ending on RS.
- On next WS row, BO 15 (17, 20) sts; work 42 (48, 53) sts in patt. On next RS and following RS rows, dec 1 st at neck edge 3 times, all sizes. Total sts on shoulder: 39 (45, 50).
- Work even in patt until 14 vertical patt repeats have been completed and the front measures 26".
- End on RS by putting sts on a storage needle for 3-needle shoulder BO.

## Right Front

- Work as for left front until 12½ vertical patt repeats have been completed, ending on WS.
- On next RS row, BO 15 (17, 20) sts; work 42 (48, 53) sts in patt. On next RS row and following RS rows, dec 1 st at neck edge 3 times, all sizes. Total sts on shoulder: 39 (45, 50).
- Work even in patt until 14 vertical repeats have been completed and the front measures 26".
- End on RS by putting shoulder sts on a storage needle for 3-needle BO.

## Sleeves

- CO 55 sts, all sizes. Work seed st patt for 2". On last WS row, inc 2 sts evenly spaced; 57 sts total.
- On next RS row begin checkerboard patt, reading chart as for back. There will be 7 horizontal repeats plus 1 st.
- On fifth and every subsequent fourth row on RS, inc 1 st each sleeve edge 27 times; 111 sts total all sizes.
- Work even in patt until 11 (12, 12) vertical patt repeats have been completed and sleeve measures 20¾ (22½, 22½)". BO all sts loosely.

## Left Front Band

Refer to "Front bands" on page 14 before picking up stitches along the front edge.

- Pick up 3 out of every 4 sts along center front edge.
- Work in seed st patt for 1½". BO loosely.

## Right Front Band

This is the buttonhole band. See "Easy buttonholes" on page 14 to plan a placement schematic for your buttonholes before starting the right front band.

- Pick up 3 out of every 4 sts on center front edge. Work in seed st for ¾". Then, following your buttonhole placement schematic for the number of buttons you have, work evenly spaced buttonholes on next RS row and following WS row. Note that the number of buttonholes should be 1 less than total number of buttons you have; reserve 1 button for the neckband.

♦ On next RS row, work again in seed st patt until buttonhole band measures 1½". BO all sts loosely.

## Neck

See "The Noble Neck" on page 13 before picking up stitches.

♦ Using 3-needle BO (see page 18), knit the front and back shoulders together.
♦ Using 1 needle, start at right front edge and pick up 2 of every 3 sts on front neck BO; pick up 1 of every 2 sts on diagonal edges; pick up 3 of every 4 sts on back neck BO and repeat the number of right front stitches on the left front. Adjust number of sts, if necessary, on left shoulder seam so that you have an odd number of stitches.
♦ Work in seed st patt for ¾".

♦ On next RS and following WS rows, work buttonhole ¾" in from front edge on right front. (See "Easy buttonholes" on page 14 for details.)
♦ On next RS row, cont in patt and work even until neckband measures 1½". BO all sts very loosely.

## Blocking

Steam without touching iron on the yarn. Stretch the body of pieces slightly to match the width of seed st bands and expand the checkerboard pattern. Alternatively, you could wash and block the pieces with slight stretch. See "Washing and blocking" on page 18 for details.

## Finishing

♦ Sew buttons to left front and neckbands, referring to "Buttons" on page 15.
♦ Sew underarm and side seams; weave in ends on reverse side.

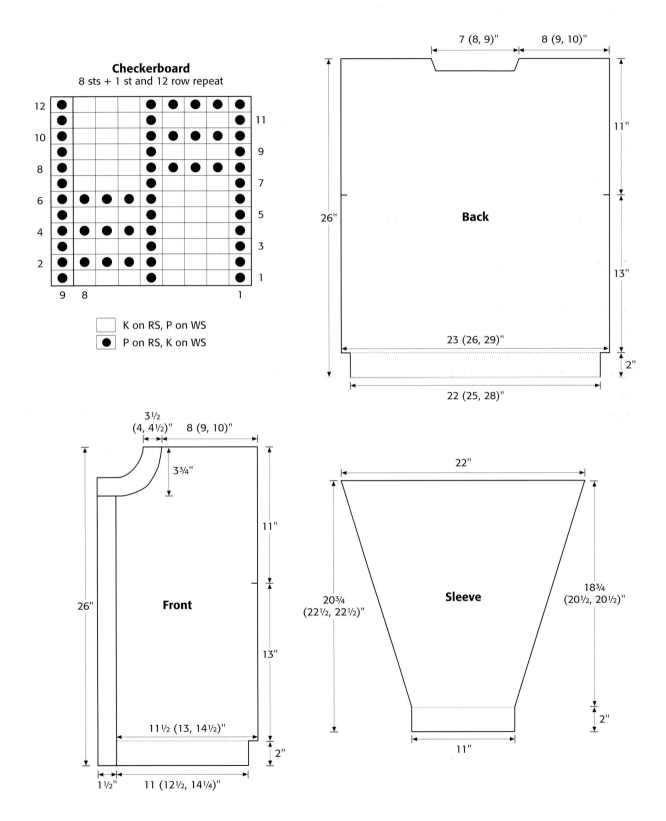

**Checkerboard**
8 sts + 1 st and 12 row repeat

☐ K on RS, P on WS
● P on RS, K on WS

# TWIST RIB
# MOCK TURTLENECK

## Designer's Notes

THIS DESIGN WITH a deep fitted ribbing uses a twist stitch to thin the tummy and waist. It also features the same deep rib on gauntlet-style sleeves and modified turtleneck. There is a striking contrast between the fitted areas that thin and the draped areas that conceal. A square armhole gives both a strong geometric line and extra roominess in the armhole because the sleeve is dovetailed into the arm opening. Even so, it is still slim enough to fit under another sweater or jacket. The sweater is meant to be worn with medium ease, neither clingy nor baggy.

Subtle hand-painted yarns are an excellent choice for this sweater, and the silky, drapey, softly-twisted DK alpaca I used takes color beautifully. Choose any luxury DK-weight yarn that drapes. I can see this pattern knit in merino or cashmere, or in a merino-silk or cashmere-silk blend. Depending on what yarn and colorway you choose, this sweater can be dressy enough for evening wear, sophisticated enough for the office, or sporty enough for weekend outings. The design is versatile and attractive on all shapes and sizes.

## Finished Measurements

To FIT SIZES: Medium (Large, XL, 1X, 2X)
FINISHED BUST: 43 (48, 52, 56, 60)"
FINISHED LENGTH: 22 (22½, 23, 23½, 24)"

## Materials

- 10 (11, 12, 13, 14) skeins of DK Weight Alpaca by America's Alpaca (100% superfine alpaca, 110 yds/50 g skein), colorway Cabin Fever
- Size 6 (4.0 mm) needles, or size to obtain gauge

## Gauge

5½ sts = 1"; 8 rows = 1" in St st

## Rib Pattern

*(Multiple of 4 sts + 2 sts)*

**Row 1:** (RS) *P2, twist 2 (Knit through back of second st on left needle; leave st on left needle; knit through front of first st on left needle; slide both sts to right needle), repeat from * to last 2 stitches, P2.
**Row 2:** (WS) K2*, P2, K2, repeat from * to end.

## Back

- CO 118 (130, 142, 154, 166) sts. Work in Rib patt for 5", ending on WS.
- On next RS row, beg St st and work for 8", ending on a WS row. With ribbing, sweater should measure 13" for all sizes.
- BO 5 (6, 7, 8, 9) sts at beg of next 2 rows for armholes; 108 (118, 128, 138, 148) sts remaining.
- Cont in St st. When armhole measures 8½ (9, 9½, 10, 10½)", on RS work 33 (36, 39, 42, 45) sts; attach second ball of yarn and BO 42 (46, 50, 54, 58) sts; work 33 (36, 39, 42, 45) sts. Cont in St st, working each side with a separate ball of yarn, until armhole measures 9 (9½, 10, 10½, 11)". BO all sts loosely.

## Front

- Work same as back until armhole measures 6½ (6¾, 7¼, 7½, 7¾)" above BO, ending on WS.
- Work 39 (42, 45, 48, 51) sts; attach second ball of yarn and BO 30 (34, 38, 42, 46) sts; work 39 (42, 45, 48, 51) sts.

♦ Cont in St st, working each side with a separate ball of yarn. On next RS row BO 2 sts on each neck edge once for all sizes; then dec 1 st each neck edge every RS row 4 times for all sizes (6 st dec total for each neck edge). Shoulders will have 33 (36, 39, 42, 45) sts.

♦ When front armholes measure 9 (9½, 10, 10½, 11)", BO all sts loosely.

## Sleeves

♦ CO 42 (46, 50, 54, 58) sts. Work in Rib patt for 3" for all sizes, ending on WS.

♦ Change to St st. At same time, on next and every subsequent fourth row (RS), inc 1 st each sleeve edge 28 (29, 30, 31, 32) times; 98 (104, 110, 116, 122) sts total.

♦ Work even in St st until sleeve measures 20 (20½, 21, 21½, 22)". BO all sts loosely.

## Neck

See "The Noble Neck" on page 13 before picking up stitches.

♦ Sew right shoulder seam. Starting on left front shoulder with straight needle, pick up on diagonal edges 1 of every 2 sts; on front neck BO, pick up 2 of every 3 sts; on back BO, pick up 3 of every 4 sts. Rib patt on neck requires a multiple of 4 sts. If necessary, make st adjustment at left shoulder.

♦ Work in Rib patt until neck measures 1½ (1¾, 2, 2¼, 2½)". BO all sts very loosely.

## Finishing

♦ No blocking is necessary. In particular, do not steam block or press ribbing.

♦ Sew left neck and shoulder seam. Sew in sleeve tops, and then sew underarm and side seams.

♦ Weave in ends on reverse side.

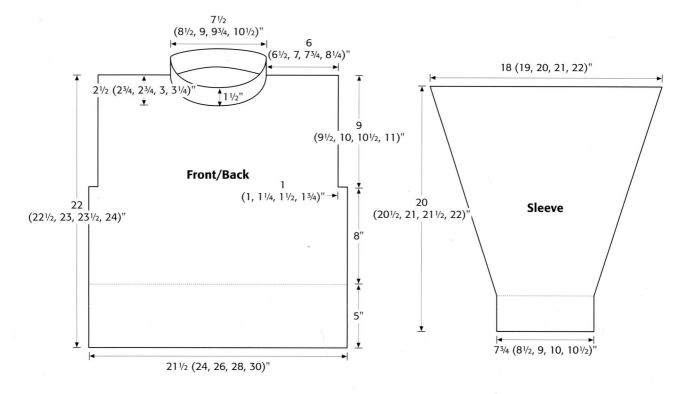

# SHAWL COLLAR
# CARDIGAN

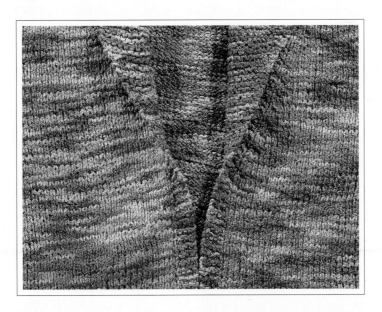

## Designer's Notes

THIS CLASSIC BUT casual design is perfect for a hand-painted yarn. I designed it to be made in cotton for three-season wear—or year-round in warm climates. However, it could just as easily be made in any fiber in the heavy worsted category that gives you the correct gauge. Silk or linen blends, wool-cotton blends, wool-silk blends, or a substantial wool would all work up quite attractively in this pattern.

The design works best with a textured yarn like the cotton bouclé used here because the knitting is very plain with lots of stockinette stitch. This sweater can easily be lengthened or shortened to suit the individual and could also be made with a ¾-length sleeve. It fits best without a front closure.

To achieve a nice fold along the collar line, short-row shaping is used in this design. If you are particularly busty or if you'd like the collar to fold back further from the face, simply add more short rows.

Another design modification that is fun and easy to do, is to knit the sweater in two colors. Knit the body of the sweater in a solid or variegated yarn, and then use a different solid color for the garter stitch edging and collar.

## Finished Measurements

SIZES: Medium (Large, XL, 1X, 2X)
FINISHED BUST: 46 (50, 54, 58, 62)"
FINISHED LENGTH: 24½ (25, 25½, 26, 26½)"

## Materials

♦ 4 (4, 5, 5, 6) skeins Cotton Bouclé (600 yds/8 oz skeins, 100% cotton) by Cherry Tree Hill Yarns, colorway Peacock
♦ Size 7 (4.5 mm) needles, or size to obtain gauge
♦ 2 stitch holders or spare needles of same or smaller size

## Gauge

4 sts = 1"; 6 rows = 1" in St st

## Back

♦ CO 92 (100, 108, 116, 124) sts. Work 8 rows garter st.
♦ On next RS row, begin St st. Work until back measures 24 (24½, 25, 25½, 26)", ending on WS.
♦ On next RS row, work 28 (32, 35, 38, 41) sts; attach second ball of yarn and BO 36 (36, 38, 40, 42) sts; work 28 (32, 35, 38, 41) sts.
♦ Cont working both shoulders on separate balls of yarn until back measures 24½ (25, 25½, 26, 26½)". BO all sts loosely.

## Left Front

♦ CO 46 (50, 54, 58, 62) sts. Work 8 rows garter st.
♦ To make garter st front band, work in the following patt. RS: Knit across; WS: K4, purl across 42 (46, 50, 54, 58) sts.
♦ Cont working this row repeat until front measures 13 (13½, 14, 14½, 15)", ending on WS.

✦ On next RS row, work to last 3 sts of St st; SSK, K1; 4 sts of garter st remain to be worked; K1, M1, K2, M1, K1. Work this dec-inc row on every fourth row on RS 14 (14, 15, 16, 17) times. St sts remaining: 28 (32, 35, 38, 41); garter sts remaining: 32 (32, 34, 36, 38).

✦ Work even on these sts until front measures 23½ (24, 24½, 25, 25½)". On last 6 rows, add 2 short rows on garter (collar) sts only every other row; total: 6 rows in St st, 12 rows in garter st. (Note: To work short rows, work only the garter sts, turn and work back. On the next row, work both the garter and St sts. Work back complete row. Repeat sequence 6 times.)

✦ On next RS row, BO 28 (32, 35, 38, 41) St sts loosely; put remaining 32 (32, 34, 36, 38) garter sts on waste yarn or holder to be finished later.

## Right Front

✦ CO 46 (50, 54, 58, 62) sts. Work 8 rows garter st to make garter st front band.

✦ Work in the following patt:
RS: Knit across
WS: purl across 42 (50, 54, 58) sts, K4.

✦ Continue working in this row repeat until front measures 13 (13½, 14, 14½, 15)" ending on WS.

✦ On next RS row (over 4 garter sts), K1, M1, K2, M1, K1. Then on St sts, which are next on needle, K1, K2tog, knit across. Work this inc-dec row on every fourth row on RS 14 (14, 15, 16, 17) times. St sts remaining: 28 (32, 35, 38, 41); garter sts remaining: 32 (32, 34, 36, 38).

✦ Work even on these sts until front measures 23½ (24, 24½, 25, 25½)". On last six rows, add 2 short rows on garter (collar) sts only every other row; total: 6 rows in St st, 12 rows in garter st. (Note: To work short rows, work only garter sts, turn and knit back. On the next row, work both the garter and St sts. Work back complete row. Repeat sequence 6 times.)

✦ On next RS row, put remaining 32 (32, 34, 36, 38) garter sts on holder, BO remaining 28 (32, 35, 38, 41) St sts loosely.

## Sleeves

✦ CO 48 (48, 50, 50, 52) sts. Work 8 rows garter st.

✦ On next RS row, begin St st.

✦ On fifth and every subsequent fourth row on RS, inc 1 st each sleeve edge 18 (20, 21, 23, 24) times; 84 (88, 92, 96, 100) sts total.

✦ Work even in St st until sleeve measures 20 (20½, 21, 21½, 22)". BO all sts loosely.

## Collar

- ✦ Sew shoulder seams. Move left collar sts from holder to needle. Work in garter st for 5 (5, 5¼, 5½, 5¾)". Leave sts on spare needle.
- ✦ Work right collar in same way. Join edges of right and left collars using 3-needle BO.

## Finishing

- ✦ Sew collar edge to back neck.
- ✦ Sew in sleeve tops; then sew underarm and side seams; weave in ends.
- ✦ After garment is finished, steam block front bands to finished dimensions.

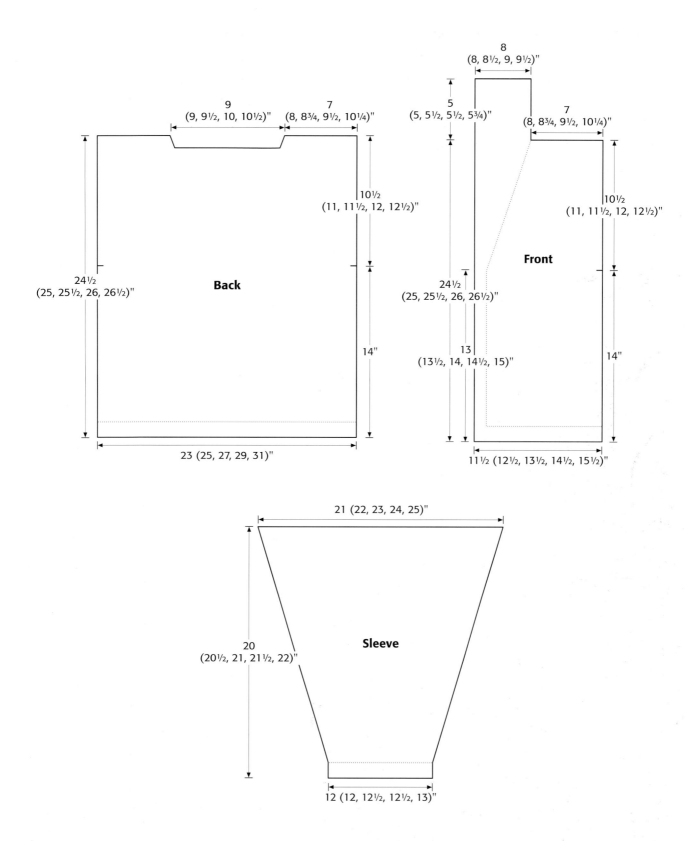

Back

9
(9, 9½, 10, 10½)"

7
(8, 8¾, 9½, 10¼)"

10½
(11, 11½, 12, 12½)"

24½
(25, 25½, 26, 26½)"

14"

23 (25, 27, 29, 31)"

8
(8, 8½, 9, 9½)"

5
(5, 5½, 5½, 5¾)"

7
(8, 8¾, 9½, 10¼)"

Front

10½
(11, 11½, 12, 12½)"

24½
(25, 25½, 26, 26½)"

13
(13½, 14, 14½, 15)"

14"

11½ (12½, 13½, 14½, 15½)"

21 (22, 23, 24, 25)"

Sleeve

20
(20½, 21, 21½, 22)"

12 (12, 12½, 12½, 13)"

# WINTER WHITE
## SHORT JACKET

## Designer's Notes

I WANTED TO design a short semi-fitted jacket in winter white that would be suitable for the office. What I came up with is this simple project that contrasts strong geometrics with a textured yarn and stitch pattern. By using matched decreases and increases on the sides, the jacket gives the illusion of being slightly fitted. For larger midriffs, the shaping could be eliminated entirely. The jacket can also be easily lengthened to suit.

The armhole is a deceptively roomy set-in square, and the lower sleeves are more fitted than the upper sleeves. Both of these design techniques are flattering on a larger figure. The square neck frames the face, and the neckline is perfect for showing off a silk scarf.

Zelda is a chunky thick-and-thin yarn. Other effects could be achieved with, say, a chunky bouclé, or Lopi. You could also use a variegated yarn, or a combination of two thinner yarns, to add color and textural interest.

The offset closure with Norwegian clasps adds a touch of sophistication. The emphasis in this design is on clean, strong lines. So, if you use a yarn that produces rough or wavy edges, as I did here, you will need to add the crochet trim to square off the edges. Choose a smooth DK-weight yarn for the crochet finish in either a matching or contrasting color.

## Finished Measurements

To FIT SIZES: Medium (Large, XL, 1X, 2X)
FINISHED BUST: 43½ (48, 52½, 56, 60½)"
FINISHED LENGTH: 22 (22½, 23, 23½, 24)"

## Materials

♦ 14 (15, 16, 17, 18) skeins Zelda (70% wool, 30% linen, 83 yds per 50 g skein) by Classic Elite, color Ivory
♦ 1 skein Inca Alpaca (100% alpaca, 116 yds per 50 g skein) by Classic Elite, color Natural, or any DK-weight yarn
♦ Size 9 (5.5 mm) needles, or size to obtain gauge
♦ Medium crochet hook
♦ 7 (7, 8, 8, 9) Norwegian clasps or number to suit
♦ Medium hook-and-eye closures

## Gauge

3.5 sts = 1", 6 rows = 1"

## Seed Stitch Pattern

*(Multiple of 2 sts)*

**All rows:** *K1, P1, repeat from * to end.

## Back

♦ CO 76 (84, 92, 98, 106) sts of Zelda. Begin patt st on first row and work in patt throughout.
♦ Dec 1 st each RS edge when sweater measures 2" and 4" (total dec 4 sts).
♦ Inc 1 st each RS edge when sweater measures 6" and 8" (total inc 4 sts).

♦ Cont in patt until back measures 13", ending on WS row.
♦ BO 8 sts at beg of next 2 rows for all sizes; sts remaining: 60 (68, 76, 82, 90). Work even until back measures 21½ (22, 22½, 23 23½)".
♦ On next RS row, work 16 (19, 23, 26, 29) sts in patt; attach second ball of yarn and BO 28 (30, 30, 30, 32) sts; work 16 (19, 23, 26, 29) sts in patt. When back measures 22 (22½, 23, 23½, 24)", BO all sts loosely.

## Left Front

♦ CO 24 (28, 32, 34, 38) sts. Work in patt until left front measures 2".
♦ On RS, dec 1 st at left edge when front measures 2" and 4" (total dec 2 sts).
♦ On RS, inc 1 st at left edge when front measures 6" and 8" (total inc 2 sts).
♦ Work even until piece measures 13", ending on a WS row.
♦ On next RS row, BO 8 sts, all sizes; sts remaining: 16 (20, 24, 26, 30).
♦ Work even until piece measures 22 (22½, 23, 23½, 24)". BO all sts loosely.

## Right Front

♦ CO 52 (56, 60, 64, 68) sts. Work in patt until right front measures 2".
♦ On RS, dec 1 st at right edge when right front measures 2" and 4" (total dec 2 sts).
♦ On RS, inc 1 st at right edge when front measures 6" and 8" (total inc 2 sts).
♦ Work even until right front measures 13", ending on RS row.

- At beg of next WS row, BO 8 sts, all sizes; sts remaining: 44 (48, 52, 56, 60).
- Work even until armhole measures 7 (7½, 8, 8½, 9)", ending on WS.
- On next RS row, BO 28 (29, 29, 30, 31) sts at left edge. Work even on 16 (19, 23, 26, 29) sts until right front measures 22 (22½, 23, 23½, 24)". BO all sts loosely.

## Sleeves

- CO 34 (38, 42, 46, 50) sts.
- Work in patt. At same time on fifth and every subsequent fourth row on RS, inc 1 st each edge 14 times, all sizes. Total sts: 62 (66, 70, 74, 78). Work even until sleeve measures 19½ (20, 20½, 21, 21½)". BO all sts loosely.

## Finishing

No blocking is required; do not steam. Dry cleaning is recommended for the yarn specified.

- Sew all pieces together with DK-weight alpaca yarn.
- With medium crochet hook and DK yarn, begin at center back and sc around entire edge, being careful not to stretch or pucker knitted edge.
- Work sc around lower sleeve edge.
- Weave in ends.
- With front opening edges flush, sew on Norwegian clasps, being careful not to leave a gap between the edges. To stabilize the join, sew a hook and eye on the inside edges of the sweater behind each clasp. Also sew a hook and eye on the inside edges halfway between each pair of clasps.

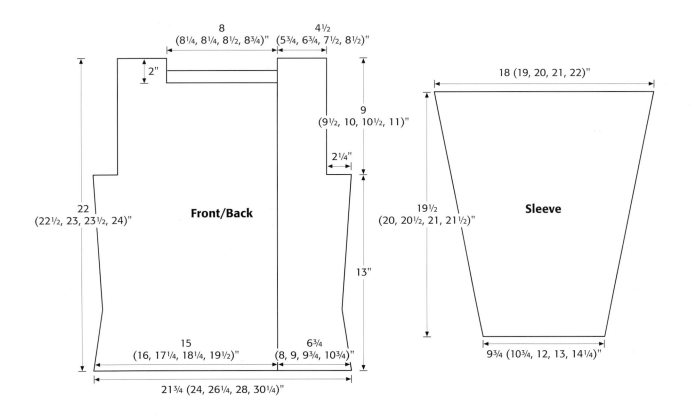

# CAT'S PAW LACE
## EVENING TOP

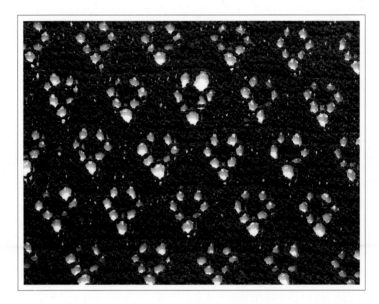

## Designer's Notes

THIS MERINO YARN works up beautifully into the traditional Shetland lace pattern called Cat's Paw. The top would also be lovely knit in silk or a silk-merino blend. Just be sure the yarn you select allows you to obtain gauge. I suggest that you choose a smooth, lustrous yarn with a good twist. Although I am partial to black, any color could be used for this design. Choosing a hand-dyed yarn, such as the Koigu used here, adds to the texture and drama of the sweater. You might even try a bolder look by using variegated yarn.

Please note that this sweater is knit to two-thirds of its full size. The finished size is achieved by blocking. To increase drape, the pieces are stretched more in length than width, so it is important to block your gauge swatch before beginning the sweater. This sweater is meant to skim the outlines of the body, not to fit tightly. It could be lined, but I would simply wear it with a silk camisole underneath.

## Finished Measurements

To FIT SIZES: Medium (Large, XL, 1X, 2X)
FINISHED BUST: 46 (50, 54, 58, 62)"
FINISHED LENGTH: 24 (25, 26, 27, 28)"

## Materials

◆ 5 (5, 6, 6, 7) skeins Koigu Premium Merino (175 yds/50 g, 100% Merino wool) by Koigu Wool Designs, color black

◆ Size 3 (3.25 mm) needles, or size to obtain gauge

## Gauge

5 st = 1"; 8 rows = 1" when blocked

## Cat's Paw Lace Pattern

*(Multiple of 8 sts + 15 sts; multiple of 20 rows)*

See chart on page 71 for pattern.

## Back

◆ CO 119 (127, 135, 143, 151) sts. Work 8 rows garter st.

◆ On next RS row, begin row 1 of lace patt. RS (odd-numbered) rows read from right to left; WS (even-numbered) rows read from left to right. Work 8 side sts, 13 (14, 15, 16, 17) 8-st repeats, and 7 side sts. Cont working even until back measures 9¼ (9½, 9¾, 10, 10¼)".

◆ On next RS row, BO 8 sts at right edge; on next WS row, BO 7 sts at left edge. Sts remaining: 104 (112, 120, 128, 136).

◆ Work even in patt until armhole above BO measures 5¼ (5½, 6½, 6½, 6½)". Work 4 rows garter st. Armhole should measure 5½ (5¾, 6½, 6½, 6¾)". BO all sts loosely.

## Front

◆ Work same as back until armhole measures 3¼ (3¼, 3½, 3½, 3½)".

◆ On next RS row, work 23 (25, 28, 31, 33) sts in patt; K2; work 54 (58, 60, 62, 66) sts garter st; all sizes work 2 sts garter st; work 23 (25, 28, 31, 33) sts in patt. Work in this manner for 3 more rows.

◆ On next RS row, work 23 (25, 28, 31, 33) sts in patt; K2. Attach second ball of yarn;

BO 54 (58, 60, 62, 66) sts; K2; work 23 (25, 28, 31, 33) sts in patt.

◆ Work each shoulder with a separate ball of yarn until armhole measures 5¼ (5½, 6¼, 6¼, 6½)".

◆ Work 4 rows garter st. Armhole should measure 5½ (5¾, 6½, 6½, 6¾)" and neck depth 2 (2¼, 2½, 2½, 2¾)". BO all sts loosely.

## Sleeves

◆ CO 63 (71, 79, 87, 95) sts. Work 8 rows garter st.

◆ On next RS row, begin lace patt. Work 8 side sts; work 6 (7, 8, 9, 10) patt repeats; work 7 side sts.

◆ On next RS and every following fourth row (RS), inc 1 st each sleeve edge 14 (12, 11, 9, 8) times; total sts: 91 (95, 101, 105, 111). Work all inc sts in garter st.

◆ Work in patt until sleeve measures 6 (6¼, 6½, 6¾, 7)". BO all sts loosely.

## Finishing

◆ Soak all pieces in tepid water overnight with no soap or detergent. The next day, roll pieces one at a time in towels to remove excess moisture. Block by stretching out and pinning piece to dimensions given in the blocked dimensions diagram on page 73. Repeat this process with each piece.

◆ When blocked pieces are thoroughly dry, sew shoulder, sleeve, underarm, and side seams. Do not steam, as this will flatten the texture.

◆ Weave in ends.

**Cat's Paw Lace Chart**

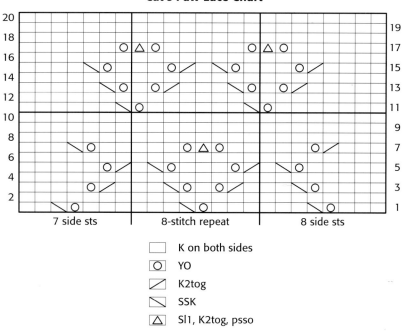

| | K on both sides |
| O | YO |
| ⟋ | K2tog |
| ⟍ | SSK |
| △ | Sl1, K2tog, psso |

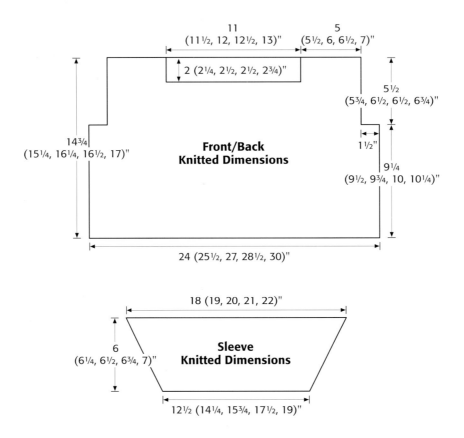

11
(11½, 12, 12½, 13)"

5
(5½, 6, 6½, 7)"

2 (2¼, 2½, 2½, 2¾)"

5½
(5¾, 6½, 6½, 6¾)"

1½"

9¼
(9½, 9¾, 10, 10¼)"

14¾
(15¼, 16¼, 16½, 17)"

**Front/Back
Knitted Dimensions**

24 (25½, 27, 28½, 30)"

18 (19, 20, 21, 22)"

6
(6¼, 6½, 6¾, 7)"

**Sleeve
Knitted Dimensions**

12½ (14¼, 15¾, 17½, 19)"

Note: Measurements are approximate based on blocked gauge.

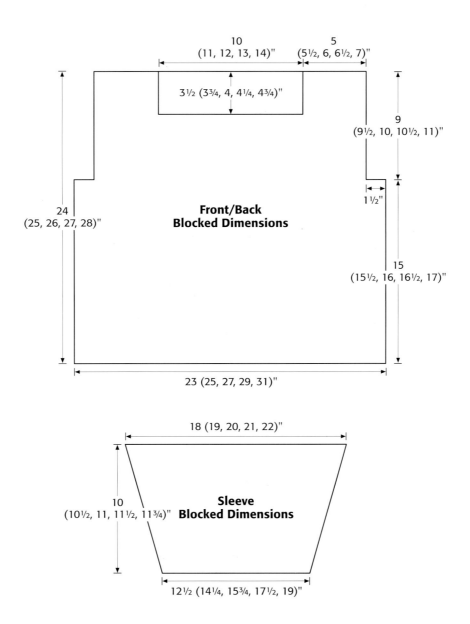

10
(11, 12, 13, 14)"

5
(5½, 6, 6½, 7)"

3½ (3¾, 4, 4¼, 4¾)"

9
(9½, 10, 10½, 11)"

1½"

24
(25, 26, 27, 28)"

**Front/Back
Blocked Dimensions**

15
(15½, 16, 16½, 17)"

23 (25, 27, 29, 31)"

18 (19, 20, 21, 22)"

10
(10½, 11, 11½, 11¾)"

**Sleeve
Blocked Dimensions**

12½ (14¼, 15¾, 17½, 19)"

# SUMMER SAGE SWEATER

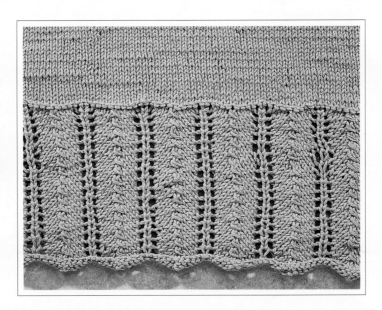

## Designer's Notes

THIS AIRY SUMMER sweater with elbow-length sleeves would look nice in any solid or tweed worsted-weight linen, cotton, or blend. Because this particular yarn is so smooth, even stitches are not necessarily desirable in the stockinette—a bit of irregularity adds texture to the sweater. Another easy way to add texture to the design is to select a bouclé yarn.

The sleeves are elbow length and loose fitting to hide heavy upper arms. If you wish to lengthen the sweater, add the rows in the lace sections rather than in the stockinette for a more interesting sweater. Rolls finish all edges.

## Finished Measurements

To FIT SIZES: Medium (Large, XL, 1X, 2X)
FINISHED BUST: 44½ (48½, 52½, 56½, 60½)"
FINISHED LENGTH: 20 (21½, 23, 24½, 26)"

## Materials

♦ 4 (5, 6, 7, 8) skeins of Cotton Fleece by Brown Sheep Yarn Company, Inc. (80% cotton, 20% merino wool, 215 yds/100 g skein), color 380 Dusty Sage.
♦ Size 6 (4.0 mm) needles, or size to obtain gauge

## Gauge

5 sts = 1"; 8 rows = 1" in St st

## Lace Pattern

*(Multiple of 10 sts + 1 st)*

**Row 1:** (RS) *Kl, YO, K3, sl1, K2tog, psso, K3, YO, repeat from*, end Kl.
**Row 2:** (WS) Purl.

## Back

♦ CO 111 (121, 131, 141, 151) sts. Work 2 rows St st; on next RS row, begin lace patt. Work in patt for 6½ (7, 7½, 8, 8½)", ending on RS row.
♦ Knit next WS row.
♦ Beg next RS row, work in St st for 4½ (5, 5½, 6, 6½)". End on WS.
♦ At beg of next 2 rows, BO 6 (7, 8, 9, 10) sts; 99 (107, 115, 123, 131) sts remaining.
♦ Work even until armhole measures 8½ (9, 9½, 10, 10½)".

♦ On next RS row, work 23 (25, 27, 29, 31) sts. Attach second ball of yarn and BO 53 (57, 61, 65, 69) sts. Work 23 (25, 27, 29, 31) sts.
♦ Work each shoulder with a separate ball of yarn until armholes measure 9 (9½, 10, 10½, 11)". BO all sts loosely.

## Front

♦ Work as for back until armhole measures 5 (5, 5, 5, 5)", ending on WS.
♦ On next row, work 31 (33, 35, 37, 39) sts. Attach second ball of yarn and BO 37 (41, 45, 49, 53) sts. Work 31 (33, 35, 37, 39) sts.
♦ Working each shoulder with a separate ball of yarn, BO 2 sts each neck edge twice. Then dec 1 st each neck edge every other row 4 times; 23 (25, 27, 29, 31) sts remaining for each shoulder.
♦ Work even in St st until armhole measures 9 (9½, 10, 10½, 11)". BO all sts loosely.

## Sleeves

♦ CO 71 (71, 81, 81, 91) sts. Work 2 rows St st, ending on WS.
♦ On next RS row, begin lace patt. Work in patt for 4¾ (5, 5¼, 5½, 5¾)", ending on RS.
♦ Knit next WS row.
♦ On next RS row, begin St st. AT SAME TIME inc 1 st each edge on fifth row and every subsequent fourth row 10 (12, 10, 12, 10) times; total sts: 91 (95, 101, 105, 111).
♦ Work even in St st until sleeve measures 11½ (12, 12½, 13, 13½)". BO all sts loosely.

## Neck

See "The Noble Neck" on page 13 before picking up stitches.

♦ Sew right shoulder seam.
♦ Starting at left front shoulder and using a straight needle, pick up 1 of every 2 sts on diagonal neck edges; pick up 2 of every 3 sts on front neck bind off; pick up 3 of every 4 sts on back neck bind off.
♦ Work 6 rows St st.
♦ BO all sts very loosely. Neck roll will show purl side when finished.

## Finishing

♦ No blocking is needed.
♦ Sew seams, using back st for stockinette edges and overcast for lace edges; weave in ends.

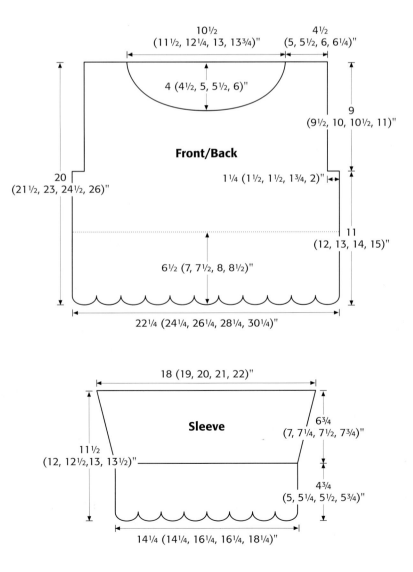

# MAJOLICA
## GANSEY PULLOVER

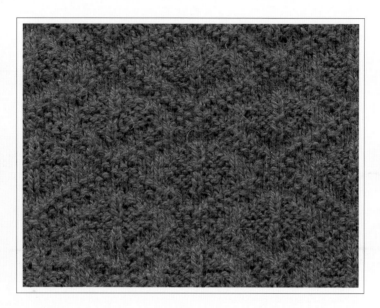

## Designer's Notes

AREN'T KNIT-PURL patterns wonderful? With two basic stitches, a whole world of design possibilities opens up for you.

I call this sweater a "gansey" because it's essentially knit-purl patterning in geometric repeats, which is of course the essence of the traditional gansey sweater. Although I have engineered it a bit differently to make it friendlier to large individuals and beginning knitters, it is basically a traditional sweater, and such classics just seem to look good on everyone.

This sweater is made in a heavy worsted-weight, llama-wool blend with lots of body and beautiful colors. Any equivalent-weight yarn could be substituted. I would, however, choose a natural fiber or fiber blend, and I do not recommend a hand-painted yarn for this design. In my opinion, wool is the best fiber for showing off textural patterns.

I have simplified the patterning on the sleeves to give a strong vertical line to the arm while still being patterned. Another trick to flatter large figures is to knit the ribbing on the same size needles as the body, to prevent it from pulling in. This works best with a K2P2 rib or patterned rib. You may have noticed that I use this technique in many of my sweaters in this book. Finally, to avoid breaking up the large pattern repeat, I have written instructions for only two sizes.

## Finished Measurements

TO FIT SIZES: Large (1X)
FINISHED BUST: 47½ (57)"
FINISHED LENGTH: 25 (28¼)"

## Materials

- 19 (24) skeins of Montera (50% llama, 50% wool, 80 yds per 50 g skein) by Classic Elite, color Majolica Blue
- Size 8 (5.0 mm) needles, or size to obtain gauge
- Set of size 8 (5.0 mm) dp needles, or size to obtain gauge

## Gauge

4.25 sts = 1", 6.5 rows = 1"

## Diamonds in Diamonds Pattern

*(Multiple of 20 sts + 1 st)*

See chart on page 81 for pattern.

## Back

- Using regular needles, CO 102 (122) sts. Work in K2P2 ribbing for 2", ending on WS.
- Purl 2 rows; dec 1 st on second purl row on WS; 101 (121) sts.
- On next RS row, begin patt from chart. Read RS (odd-numbered) rows from left to right; read WS (even-numbered) rows from right to left. Work 5 (6) horizontal repeats plus 1 st across: 101 (121) sts.

- Work even in patt until 7 (8) vertical patt repeats plus 1 row have been completed. Back should measure 25 (28¼)" in length. BO all sts loosely.

## Front

- Work as for back until 6 (7) vertical patt repeats have been completed, ending on WS.
- On next RS row, in patt, work across 38 (44) sts; attach second ball of yarn and BO 25 (33) sts; work 38 (44) sts in patt.
- On next RS row, dec 1 st each neck edge 4 times both sizes, 34 (40) sts for each shoulder. Cont in patt until front measures 25 (28¼)" and 7 (8) vertical patt repeats plus 1 row have been completed. BO all sts loosely.

## Sleeves

- CO 48 (52) sts. Work K2P2 ribbing for 2", ending on WS.
- Purl 2 rows, decreasing 1 st on last purl row; 47 (51) sts.
- On next RS row, begin patt as follows: K3 (5) sts; work 2 horizontal patt repeats plus 1 st (41 sts); K3 (5) sts.
- On fifth row (RS) and every subsequent fourth row, inc 1 st each edge in St st 15 (25) times. Work even in patt on 77 (101) sts until 5 (6) vertical repeats plus 1 row have been completed and sleeve measures 18½ (21¾)" from beg. BO all sts loosely.

## Neck

See "The Noble Neck" on page 13 before picking up stitches.

◆ Sew shoulder seams.
◆ Using dp needles, pick up 1 of every 2 sts on diagonal edges; 2 of every 3 sts on front neck BO; 3 of every 4 sts on back neck BO. K2P2 ribbing is a 4 st repeat. If necessary, adjust number of sts on left shoulder.
◆ Work in rib patt in the round for 1". BO all sts very loosely.

## Finishing

◆ No blocking is necessary.
◆ Sew all seams; weave in ends.
◆ Do not steam, as this will flatten the pattern sts.

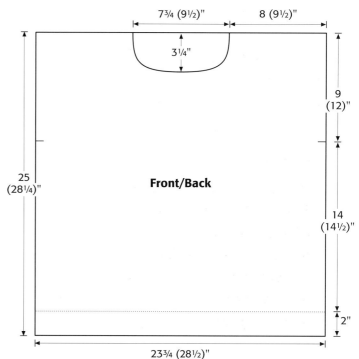

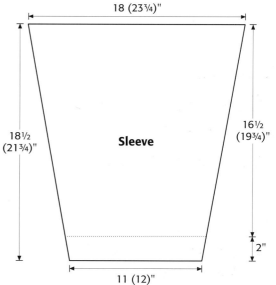

**Gansey Stitch Chart**
20 sts and 20 row repeat

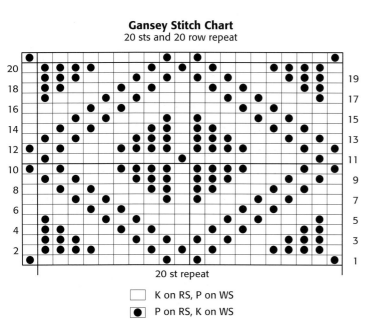

20 st repeat

□ K on RS, P on WS
● P on RS, K on WS

# SOFT AND LACY

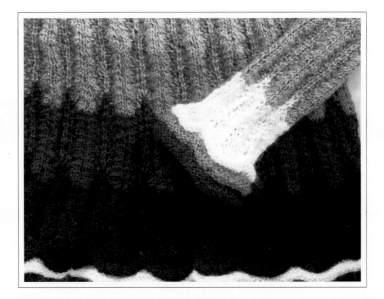

## Designer's Notes

AT HEART, I am a Shetland lace knitter! Soft and Lacy combines colors with the Shetland Old Shell lace pattern and features the new longer, draped cuffs. The heavy fingering-weight yarn is a super-soft, luxurious mohair-wool blend that provides a rich color palette and takes a lace pattern very well. Shading is the important feature of this color scheme—I used five colors. If you choose your own color scheme, keep in mind the goal of shading from light to dark. And that does not necessarily mean it has to be made from shades of a single color.

If you choose another yarn, I would suggest cashmere, cashmere-silk, cashmere-merino, or merino-silk blend. You basically need a very soft, medium-twist, nonhairy yarn for this design. I think this sweater really cries out for a special luxury fiber; I would not recommend angora, pure mohair, acrylic, or cotton.

Putting the darkest color on the hips and using a neutral body color are thinning, as is the general verticality of the lace pattern. The color bands add only a token horizontal element. The lines of the sweater and sleeve are long and fitted. This sweater is meant to be semi-fitted, but not tight. It should be body skimming. The two sizes cover a lot of body dimensions, and because the lace is stretchy, you can block it to your own taste in fit. I would wear this sweater for special occasions, as it is quite dressy.

## Finished Measurements

To FIT SIZES: Large (1X)
FINISHED BUST: 47 (56)"
FINISHED LENGTH: 26"

## Materials

- ◆ Tiur (60% mohair, 40% wool, 126 yds per 50 gm skein) by Dale of Norway in the following quantities and colors:
  **Color A:** 12 (16) skeins Gray
  **Color B:** 2 (4) skeins White
  **Color C:** 2 (4) skeins Light Blue
  **Color D:** 2 (4) skeins Medium Navy Blue
  **Color E:** 2 (4) skeins Dark Navy Blue
- ◆ Size 3 (3.25 mm) needles, or size to obtain gauge

## Gauge

6 sts = 1"; 8 rows = 1" in lace pattern

## Lace Pattern

*(Multiple of 14 sts + 1 st; multiple of 2 rows)*

See chart on page 87 for lace pattern.

## Back

- ◆ In color E, CO 141 (169) sts.
- ◆ Work 2 rows St st; work 4 rows reverse St st; work 2 rows St st.
- ◆ Change to B and repeat 8-row sequence.
- ◆ Change to E and repeat 8-row sequence.
- ◆ On next RS row, begin lace patt using chart on page 87, reading RS (odd-numbered rows) from right to left and WS (even-numbered rows) from left to right. Work 10 (12) horizontal patterns plus 1 st. Work even in lace patt until lace above rolled edging measures 3".
- ◆ Change to D and knit in lace patt for 3".
- ◆ Change to C and knit in lace patt for 3".
- ◆ Change to A and knit in lace patt until entire piece measures 25½".
- ◆ On next RS row, work 43 (57) sts in patt; attach second ball of yarn and BO 55 sts; work 43 (57) sts in patt.
- ◆ On next RS row, dec 1 st each neck edge once. Total sts on each shoulder: 42 (56). When piece measures 26", BO all sts loosely.

## Front

♦ Work as for back until piece measures 23" from bottom edge. You are in the A color area.

♦ On next RS row, work 44 (58) sts in patt; attach second ball of yarn and BO 53 sts; work 44 (58) sts in patt.

♦ On next RS row, dec 1 st each neck edge twice. Total sts on each shoulder: 42 (56) sts.

♦ Working each side with a separate ball of yarn, work even in lace patt until piece measures 26". BO all sts loosely.

## Sleeves

♦ In color D, CO 57 sts. Work 2 rows St st; work 4 rows reverse St st; work 2 rows St st.

♦ Change to C and repeat 8-row sequence.

♦ Change to B and repeat 8-row sequence.

♦ Continuing in B, on next RS row, begin lace patt, reading chart as for back. Work 4 horizontal 14-st repeats plus 1 st. Work lace patt in B for 3" from top of rolled edge. AT THE SAME TIME, on fifth and every subsequent fourth row on RS, inc 1 st each sleeve edge 29 (35) times in St st. Total sts: 115 (127).

♦ After 3" of B, change to A and work even in patt until sleeve measures 22 (24)" from bottom edge. BO all sts loosely.

## Neck

See "The Noble Neck" on page 13 before picking up stitches.

♦ Sew right shoulder seam. With 1 straight needle, starting at left shoulder, pick up 1 of every 2 sts on diagonals; pick up 2 of every 3 sts on front neck BO; pick up 3 of every 4 sts on back neck BO. This neck requires 113 sts to accommodate 8 lace patt repeats plus 1 st, so make adjustments evenly spaced on first row to arrive at this total. Total neck circumference will be 19".

♦ Work back and forth in B in St st until neck measures 3½". Purl 2 rows for fold.

♦ Switching RS and WS so inside of neck will be face out when you fold it over, work in lace patt for 2½" from fold.

♦ Change to A and work 2 rows St st; work 4 rows reverse St st; work 2 rows St st.

♦ Change to B and repeat 8-row sequence. BO all sts very loosely.

## Finishing

♦ Sew shoulder and neck seams. Neck seam will be on inside of neck on St st section and outside of unfolded neck on lace section. Fold neck.

♦ Sew rest of seams; weave in ends.

♦ After finishing seams, steam and stretch slightly to block, but do not put iron down on surface, as this will flatten patt.

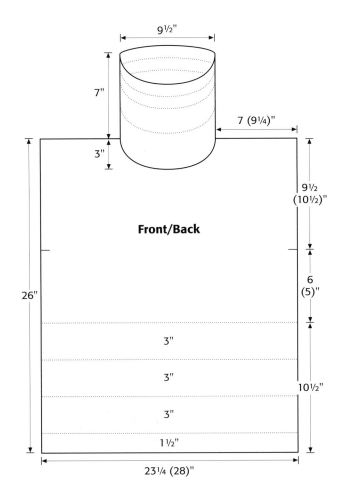

9½"

7"

3"

7 (9¼)"

9½
(10½)"

**Front/Back**

6
(5)"

26"

3"

3"

10½"

3"

1½"

23¼ (28)"

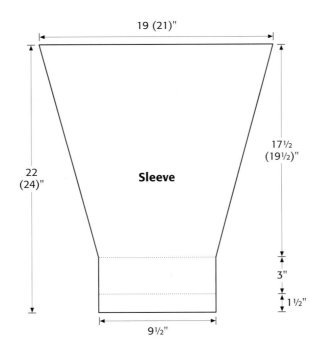

19 (21)"

Sleeve

22 (24)"

17½ (19½)"

3"

1½"

9½"

## Shetland Old Shell Lace Variation
14 sts plus 1 st and 2 row repeat

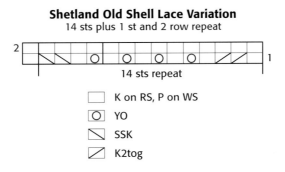

2

1

14 sts repeat

☐  K on RS, P on WS

◯  YO

◿  SSK

◹  K2tog

# ABBREVIATIONS FOR COMMON KNITTING TERMS

| | |
|---|---|
| **approx** | approximately |
| **beg** | beginning |
| **BO** | bind off |
| **C** | cable |
| **CC** | contrasting color |
| **ch** | chain |
| **circ** | circular |
| **cn** | cable needle |
| **CO** | cast on |
| **cont** | continue |
| **dec** | decrease |
| **DK** | double knitting yarn, the designation for yarn slightly thicker than sport weight |
| **dp** | double pointed (as in *double-pointed needles*) |
| **EOR** | every other row |
| **g** | gram |
| **inc** | increase |
| **K** | knit |
| **K2tog** | knit 2 together |
| **K2tog tbl** | knit 2 together through the back loop |

| | |
|---|---|
| **M1** | Make 1 stitch: lift horizontal thread between 2 stitches and place loop on left-hand needle; work new stitch through back loop |
| **MC** | main color |
| **oz** | ounces |
| **P** | purl |
| **psso** | pass slipped stitch(es) over |
| **pw** | purl wise |
| **rep** | repeat |
| **RS** | right side |
| **RSR** | right side row |
| **sc** | single crochet |
| **sl** | slip |
| **SSK** | slip, slip, knit |
| **SSP** | slip, slip, purl |
| **st(s)** | stitch(es) |
| **St st** | stockinette stitch |
| **tog** | together |
| **wyib** | with yarn in back |
| **wyif** | with yarn in front |
| **WS** | wrong side |
| **YO** | yarn over |

# ACKNOWLEDGMENTS

I WANT TO thank Martingale & Company and, in particular, Mary Green and Karen Soltys for their encouragement and professionalism. My husband has been my biggest supporter. He prepared the manuscript and was consulted on many aspects of the book. Claudia Judson Chesney was my sounding board and knitted the Mohair Cable Pullover and Winter White Short Jacket. Her suggestions were always helpful. The love and support of my family were vital to me, as always. Margaret Dalrymple was there for me, both personally and professionally, from the development of the original idea to the production of the finished book. Thank you Galina Khmeleva for not letting any grass grow under my feet.

# GUIDE TO SUPPLIERS

PLEASE CONTACT THE following yarn companies for a list of suppliers in your area.

AMERICA'S ALPACA
6555 State Highway 30E
Decatur, TN 37322
www.americasalpaca.com

BROWN SHEEP COMPANY
100662 Country Road 16
Mitchell, NE 69357
www.brownsheep.com

CHERRY TREE HILL YARN
52 Church Street
Barton, VT 05822
www.cherryyarn.com

CLASSIC ELITE YARNS
300 Jackson Street
Lowell, MA 01852
classicelite@aol.com

DALE OF NORWAY
N16 W23390 Stoneridge Drive
Suite A
Waukesha, WI 53188
www.dale.no

KOIGU WOOL DESIGNS
R.R. #1
Williamsford, Ontario
NOH 2VO Canada
www.koigu.com

# ABOUT THE AUTHOR

Carol Rasmussen Noble is a knitwear designer, author, and textile collector who has been knitting since the age of eight. Her previous books are *Gossamer Webs: The History and Techniques of Orenburg Shawls* and *Knitting Fair Isle Mittens and Gloves*. Mrs. Noble lives in Reno, Nevada, with her husband and cat.

# new and bestselling titles from

America's Best-Loved Knitting Books®

America's Best-Loved Quilt Books®

---

## NEW RELEASES
20 Decorated Baskets
Asian Elegance
Batiks and Beyond
Classic Knitted Vests
Clever Quilts Encore
Crocheted Socks!
Four Seasons of Quilts
Happy Endings
Judy Murrah's Jacket Jackpot
Knits for Children and Their Teddies
Loving Stitches
Meadowbrook Quilts
Once More around the Block
Pairing Up
Patchwork Memories
Pretty and Posh
Professional Machine Quilting
Purely Primitive
Shadow Appliqué
Snowflake Follies
Style at Large
Trashformations
World of Quilts, A

## APPLIQUÉ
Appliquilt in the Cabin
Artful Album Quilts
Blossoms in Winter
Color-Blend Appliqué
Garden Party
Sunbonnet Sue All through the Year

## HOLIDAY QUILTS & CRAFTS
Christmas Cats and Dogs
Christmas Delights
Creepy Crafty Halloween
Handcrafted Christmas, A
Hocus Pocus!
Make Room for Christmas Quilts
Snowman's Family Album Quilt, A
Welcome to the North Pole

## LEARNING TO QUILT
101 Fabulous Rotary-Cut Quilts
Casual Quilter, The
Fat Quarter Quilts
More Fat Quarter Quilts
Quick Watercolor Quilts
Quilts from Aunt Amy
Simple Joys of Quilting, The
Your First Quilt Book (or it should be!)

## PAPER PIECING
40 Bright and Bold Paper-Pieced Blocks
50 Fabulous Paper-Pieced Stars
Down in the Valley
Easy Machine Paper Piecing
For the Birds
It's Raining Cats and Dogs
Papers for Foundation Piecing
Quilter's Ark, A
Show Me How to Paper Piece
Traditional Quilts to Paper Piece

## QUILTS FOR BABIES & CHILDREN
Easy Paper-Pieced Baby Quilts
Even More Quilts for Baby
More Quilts for Baby
Play Quilts
Quilts for Baby
Sweet and Simple Baby Quilts

## ROTARY CUTTING/SPEED PIECING
101 Fabulous Rotary-Cut Quilts
365 Quilt Blocks a Year Perpetual Calendar
1000 Great Quilt Blocks
Around the Block Again
Around the Block with Judy Hopkins
Cutting Corners
Log Cabin Fever
Pairing Up
Strips and Strings
Triangle-Free Quilts
Triangle Tricks

## SCRAP QUILTS
Nickel Quilts
Rich Traditions
Scrap Frenzy
Spectacular Scraps
Successful Scrap Quilts

## TOPICS IN QUILTMAKING
Americana Quilts
Bed and Breakfast Quilts
Bright Quilts from Down Under
Creative Machine Stitching
Everyday Embellishments
Fabulous Quilts from Favorite Patterns
Folk Art Friends
Handprint Quilts
Just Can't Cut It!
Quilter's Home: Winter, The
Split-Diamond Dazzlers
Time to Quilt

## CRAFTS
300 Papermaking Recipes
ABCs of Making Teddy Bears, The
Blissful Bath, The
Creating with Paint
Handcrafted Frames
Handcrafted Garden Accents
Painted Whimsies
Pretty and Posh
Sassy Cats
Stamp in Color

## KNITTING & CROCHET
365 Knitting Stitches a Year
   Perpetual Calendar
Basically Brilliant Knits
Crochet for Tots
Crocheted Aran Sweaters
Knitted Sweaters for Every Season
Knitted Throws and More
Knitter's Template, A
Knitting with Novelty Yarns
More Paintbox Knits
Simply Beautiful Sweaters for Men
Today's Crochet
Too Cute! Cotton Knits for Toddlers
Treasury of Rowan Knits, A
Ultimate Knitter's Guide, The

---

Our books are available at bookstores and your favorite craft, fabric, and yarn retailers. If you
don't see the title you're looking for, visit us at **www.martingale-pub.com** or contact us at:

## 1-800-426-3126

International: 1-425-483-3313 • Fax: 1-425-486-7596 • Email: info@martingale-pub.com

For more information and a full list of our titles, visit our Web site.